Congressional Research Service

DNA Testing in Criminal Justice: Background, Current Law, Grants, and Issues

Nathan James
Analyst in Crime Policy

December 6, 2012

Congressional Research Service

7-5700

www.crs.gov

R41800

CRS Report for Congress ————————————————

Prepared for Members and Committees of Congress

Summary

Deoxyribonucleic acid, or DNA, is the fundamental building block for an individual's entire genetic makeup. DNA is a powerful tool for law enforcement investigations because each person's DNA is different from that of every other individual (except for identical twins). DNA can be extracted from a number of sources, such as hair, bone, teeth, saliva, and blood. As early as the 1980s, states began enacting laws that required collecting DNA samples from offenders convicted of certain sexual and other violent crimes. The samples were then analyzed and their profiles entered into state databases. Meanwhile, the Federal Bureau of Investigation (FBI) Laboratory convened a working group of federal, state, and local forensic scientists to establish guidelines for the use of forensic DNA analysis in laboratories. The group proposed guidelines that are the basis of current national quality assurance standards, and it urged the creation of a national DNA database. The criminal justice community began to utilize DNA analyses more often in criminal investigations and trials, and in 1994 Congress enacted legislation to authorize the creation of a national DNA database.

Federal law (42 U.S.C §14132(a)) authorizes the FBI to operate and maintain a national DNA database where DNA profiles generated from samples collected from people under applicable legal authority and samples collected at crime scenes can be compared to generate leads in criminal investigations. Statutory provisions also authorize the collection of DNA samples from federal offenders and arrestees, District of Columbia offenders, and military offenders. State laws dictate which convicted offenders, and sometimes people arrested for crimes, will have profiles entered into state DNA databases, while federal law dictates the scope of the national database. Increasing awareness of the power of DNA to solve crimes has resulted in increased demand for DNA analysis, which has resulted in a backlog of casework. Some jurisdictions have started to use their DNA databases for familial searching, which involves using offender profiles to identify relatives who might be perpetrators of crimes. In addition to solving crimes, DNA analysis can help exonerate people incarcerated for crimes they did not commit.

Congress has authorized several grant programs to provide assistance to state and local governments for forensic sciences. Many of the programs focus on providing state and local governments with funding to reduce the backlog of forensic and convicted offender DNA samples waiting to be processed and entered into the national database. Since FY2006, Congress has appropriated approximately $785 million for backlog reduction and laboratory capacity enhancement programs. However, other grant programs provide funding for related purposes, such as offsetting the cost of providing post-conviction DNA testing.

In the 1990s and the early part of the last decade, most of the debate in Congress focused on the scope of DNA databases, reducing the backlog of DNA casework, and providing access to post-conviction DNA testing. Most of the debate about the scope of DNA databases faded away with the enactment of the Violence Against Women and Department of Justice Reauthorization Act of 2005 (P.L. 109-162), which expanded federal collection statutes to include anyone arrested or detained under the authority of the United States. The act also expanded the scope of the national database to include DNA profiles of individuals arrested for state crimes. However, concerns about the backlog of DNA casework and access to post-conviction testing have persisted. In addition, new issues related to the use of DNA in criminal justice have emerged, including whether (1) DNA databases should be used to conduct familial searches, (2) sexual assault evidence collection kits (i.e., "rape kits") should be standardized, and (3) there should be national accreditation standards for forensic laboratories.

Contents

Introduction.. 1

Background 2

    The National DNA Index System (NDIS) and the Combined DNA Index System
      (CODIS) 2

    DNA Profiles 3

    Collection of DNA Samples from State Offenders.. 7

    DNA Backlog 8

        Forensic Casework 8

        Convicted Offender and Arrestee Samples.. 10

        Evidence in the Possession of Law Enforcement... 11

        Processing Time for DNA Analyses.. 12

        Sexual Assault Evidence Collection Kits 12

    Investigation of Leads Generated from Database Hits 14

    Partial Match Searching 15

    Post-conviction DNA Testing 16

Current Federal Statutory Law 17

    Quality Assurance and Proficiency Testing Standards 18

    Index to Facilitate Law Enforcement Exchange of DNA Identification Information 18

    Collection of DNA Samples from Certain Federal, District of Columbia, and Military
      Offenders 20

    Post-conviction DNA Testing 21

    Preservation of Biological Evidence 24

Grants for DNA-Related Programs 24

    Debbie Smith DNA Backlog Grant Program 24

    Kirk Bloodsworth Post-Conviction DNA Testing Grant Program 25

    Sexual Assault Forensic Exam Program Grants 26

    DNA Research and Development Grants 26

    DNA Training and Education for Law Enforcement, Correctional Personnel, and
      Court Officers.. 26

    Appropriations for DNA-Related Grant Programs... 26

Selected Legislative Issues for Congress... 27

    The NDIS and Familial Searching... 28

    Reducing the Backlog... 31

        Enhancing the Capacity of State and Local Laboratories 32

        Facilitating Partnerships Between Public and Private Laboratories................................... 34

    Annual Backlog Data 36

    Standardization of Sexual Assault Evidence Collection Kits 37

    Arrestee Collection Statutes 39

    Access to Post-conviction Testing... 40

    Federal Accreditation Standards.. 40

Figures

Figure 1. DNA Forensic Casework: Supply, Demands, Backlogs... 9

Figure 2. Convicted Offender and Arrestee Backlog Trends, 2007-2009 11

Tables

Table 1. Number of Profiles in the NDIS, Investigations Aided, and Hits Generated by
    Searches of NDIS 6

Table 2. Appropriations for Forensic Science Grant Programs 27

Table A-1. State DNA Database Laws, Qualifying Offenses 42

Appendixes

Appendix. State DNA Database Laws 42

Contacts

Author Contact Information 45

Introduction

Deoxyribonucleic acid, or DNA, is the fundamental building block for an individual's entire genetic makeup. DNA is a powerful tool for law enforcement investigations because each person's DNA is different from that of every other individual (except for identical twins). By analyzing selected DNA sequences (called loci), a crime laboratory can develop a profile to be used in identifying a suspect.[1]

DNA can be extracted from a number of sources, such as hair, bone, teeth, saliva, and blood. Because the human body contains so many copies of DNA, even a minuscule amount of bodily fluid or tissue can yield useful information. Obtaining a DNA sample is not necessarily invasive; it can be as simple as a swab of the inside of the mouth to obtain saliva.

State and federal DNA databases have proved instrumental in solving crimes, reducing the risk of convicting the wrong person, and establishing the innocence of those wrongly convicted. DNA evidence is used to solve crimes in two ways:

- In cases where a suspect is known, a sample of that person's DNA can be compared to biological evidence found at a crime scene. The results of this comparison may then help establish whether the suspect was at the crime scene or whether he/she committed the crime.[2]

- In cases where a suspect is not known, biological evidence from the crime scene can be analyzed and compared to offender profiles contained in existing DNA databases to assist in identifying the perpetrator.[3] Through the use of DNA databases, biological evidence found at one crime scene can also be connected to other crime scenes, linking them to the same perpetrator or perpetrators.[4]

Early congressional debate on DNA testing centered on whose profiles should be included in DNA databases. In recent years, concerns have been raised about the backlog of DNA casework and access to post-conviction testing. In the future, policymakers may also focus their attention on other issues related to the use of DNA in criminal justice, including whether (1) DNA databases should be used to conduct familial searches, (2) sexual assault evidence collection kits (i.e., "rape kits") should be standardized, and (3) there should be national accreditation standards for forensic laboratories.

This report provides an overview of how DNA is used to investigate crimes and help protect the innocent.[5] It also reviews current statutory law on collecting DNA samples, sharing DNA profiles

---

[1] See CRS Report RL30717, *DNA Identification: Applications and Issues*, by Eric A. Fischer.

[2] U.S. Department of Justice, *DNA Initiative: Possible Results from DNA Tests*, http://www.dna.gov/basics/analysis/types-of-results.

[3] U.S. Department of Justice, *DNA Initiative: Forensic DNA Databases*, http://www.dna.gov/dna-databases/.

[4] Ibid.

[5] This report does not include a discussion of the use of DNA to identify missing persons and unidentified human remains, nor does it include an overview of grant programs to state and local governments for developing DNA profiles from samples from missing persons, close relatives of missing persons, or unidentified human remains. For more on this issue, see CRS Report RL34616, *Missing Adults: Background, Federal Programs, and Issues for Congress*, by Adrienne L. Fernandes-Alcantara.

---

generated from those samples, and providing access to post-conviction DNA testing. The report also includes a summary of grant programs authorized by Congress to assist state and local governments with reducing DNA backlogs, provide post-conviction DNA testing, and promote new technology in the field. It also reviews select issues Congress might consider should it legislate or conduct oversight in this area.

Background

Federal law authorizes the Federal Bureau of Investigation (FBI) to operate and maintain a national DNA database where DNA profiles generated from samples collected from people under applicable legal authority and samples collected at crime scenes can be compared to generate leads in criminal investigations. Statutory provisions also authorize the collection of DNA samples from federal offenders and arrestees, District of Columbia offenders, and military offenders. State law dictates which convicted offenders and persons arrested for crimes will have profiles entered into state DNA databases, but federal law dictates which profiles entered into state databases can be uploaded into the national DNA database.

Increasing awareness of the power of DNA testing to solve crimes has increased demand for DNA analysis, which has resulted in a backlog of casework. The demonstrated ability of DNA testing to generate leads in criminal investigations has led some jurisdictions to use their DNA databases for familial searching, which involves using offender profiles to identify relatives who might be perpetrators of crimes. In addition to solving crimes, DNA analysis can also help exonerate people incarcerated for crimes they did not commit.

The National DNA Index System (NDIS) and the Combined DNA Index System (CODIS)

As early as the 1980s, states began enacting laws that required DNA samples from those offenders convicted of certain sexual offenses and other violent crimes. The samples were then analyzed and their profiles entered into state databases. Meanwhile, the FBI Laboratory convened a working group of federal, state, and local forensic scientists to establish guidelines for the use of forensic DNA analysis in laboratories. The group proposed guidelines that are the basis of current national quality assurance standards, and it urged the creation of a national DNA database.[6] In 1994, Congress authorized the FBI to establish and oversee the National DNA Index System (NDIS). When the NDIS launched in 1998, only nine states participated.[7] Currently, laboratories in all 50 states, the District of Columbia, the federal government, Puerto Rico, and the U.S. Army Criminal Investigation Laboratory participate in the NDIS.[8] The NDIS contains the DNA profiles

---

[6] Statement of Dwight E. Adams, Deputy Assistant Director, Laboratory Division, Federal Bureau of Investigation, in U.S. Congress, House of Representatives, Government Reform Committee, Subcommittee on Government Efficiency, Financial Management and Intergovernmental Relations, *How Effective are State and Federal Agencies Working Together to Implement the Use of New DNA Technologies?*, hearing, 107th Cong., 1st sess., March 29, 2004, pp. 53-54, at http://www.fbi.gov/congress/congress01/dwight061201.htm.

[7] John M. Butler, *Fundamentals of Forensic DNA Typing* (Burlington, MA: Academic Press, 2010), p. 265 (hereafter, *Fundamentals of Forensic DNA Typing*).

[8] Ibid.

provided by federal, state, and participating local crime laboratories.[9] As of January 2011, there are 198 laboratories in the United States participating in the NDIS.[10]

DNA profiles generated by laboratories operated by local law enforcement agencies are stored in Local DNA Index Systems (LDIS). DNA profiles generated by state laboratories, along with authorized profiles stored in participating LDIS, are uploaded into State DNA Index Systems (SDIS). Each state has its own laws specifying which profiles can be included in the SDIS. DNA profiles generated by federal laboratories, along with authorized DNA profiles in participating SDIS, are uploaded into the NDIS.[11] Federal law dictates which DNA profiles can be stored in the NDIS (see below). The NDIS allows participating laboratories to compare DNA on the national level while the SDIS allows each state to compare DNA profiles stored at the state level. Federal, state, and local laboratories upload and compare DNA profiles using the Combined DNA Index System (CODIS) software produced and distributed by the FBI.[12]

CODIS searches three indexes (convicted offenders, arrestee, and forensic) to generate investigative leads. The convicted offender index contains DNA profiles developed from samples collected from convicted offenders; the arrestee index contains DNA profiles developed from samples collected from arrested but *not yet convicted* individuals; and the forensic index contains DNA profiles developed from samples collected at crime scenes. CODIS searches across these indexes to look for potential matches (also referred to as "hits").[13] Matches can occur between either the convicted offender or arrestee indexes and the forensic index, thereby providing law enforcement with the identity of one or more suspects.[14] Also, matches can occur between DNA profiles in the forensic index, thereby linking crime scenes to each other and identifying serial offenders.[15] Matches between multiple samples in the forensic index can allow law enforcement agencies in different jurisdictions to coordinate their efforts and share leads. No names or other personal identifiers for offender and arrestee DNA profiles are stored in the NDIS, so when a match is made in CODIS, the laboratories that submitted the DNA profiles to the NDIS are notified of the match and they contact each other to verify the match and coordinate their efforts.[16]

DNA Profiles

DNA profiles entered into CODIS are based on 13 core short tandem repeat (STR) loci selected by the FBI.[17] The FBI chose 13 core loci to ensure that all forensic laboratories can establish uniform DNA databases and share forensic information through the NDIS.[18] Currently, the 13

---

[9] U.S. Department of Justice, Federal Bureau of Investigation, *Fact Sheet—CODIS and the National DNA Index System*, http://www.fbi.gov/about-us/lab/codis/codis-and-ndis-fact-sheet (hereafter "CODIS Fact Sheet").

[10] U.S. Department of Justice, Federal Bureau of Investigation, *CODIS—NDIS Statistics*, http://www.fbi.gov/about-us/lab/codis/ndis-statistics.

[11] Ibid.

[12] U.S. Department of Justice, *DNA Initiative: DNA Databases*, http://www.dna.gov/dna-databases/levels.

[13] Ibid.

[14] Ibid. If an "offender hit" is obtained, that information typically is used as probable cause to obtain a new DNA sample from that suspect so the match can be confirmed by the crime laboratory before an arrest is made.

[15] Ibid.

[16] CODIS Fact Sheet.

[17] Ibid.

[18] U.S. Department of Justice, *DNA Initiative: About Forensic DNA*, http://www.dna.gov/basics/analysis/str.

STR loci used by the FBI are non-coding, meaning that they have not been shown to be associated with human attributes such as height, eye or skin color, or susceptibility to a particular disease.[19] Each locus has two alleles, and it is these 13 pairs of alleles that are compared to match samples in the forensic index with profiles in either the offender or arrestee indexes. The 13 core loci chosen by the FBI provide a high level of discriminatory power. The probability that two unrelated individuals would share all 13 pairs of alleles is estimated to be one in several hundred billion.[20] Two random Americans will, on average, share two or three alleles.[21]

It is important to ensure the quality of the DNA profiles entered into the NDIS. If the profiles are not accurate, they are of little use for making matches between forensic and offender or arrestee profiles. The FBI helps ensure the quality of DNA profiles included in the NDIS by signing memorandums of understanding with state laboratories whereby the laboratory agrees to adhere to the FBI's Quality Assurance Standards (QAS, see below).[22] Laboratories submitting DNA profiles to the NDIS must be accredited and audited annually.[23] Annual audits can be conducted by either an internal or external auditor, but laboratories must be audited by an external agency at least once every two years.[24] Laboratories that do not pass the annual audit can be prevented from entering DNA profiles in CODIS.[25] Currently, most labs in the United States are audited by the American Society of Crime Laboratory Directors and its Laboratory Accreditation Board (ASCLD/LAB) and Forensic Quality Services (FQS). In addition, DNA analysts must undergo semiannual proficiency testing.[26] DNA analysts who do not pass their semiannual proficiency tests are not allowed to enter profiles into CODIS.[27] Laboratories are also required to conduct two reviews of all DNA profiles before they are entered into CODIS.[28]

Currently, as prescribed by federal law (see below), only public laboratories that comply with the QAS can submit DNA profiles to the NDIS. However, public laboratories are allowed to outsource casework to private laboratories. Data from the Bureau of Justice Statistics (BJS) of the Department of Justice show that public laboratories are outsourcing more work to private laboratories. BJS reports that 28% of public laboratories reported that they outsourced DNA

---

[19] Jules Epstein, "Genetic Surveillance—The *Bogeyman* Response to Familial DNA Investigations," *University of Illinois Journal of Law, Technology and Policy*, vol. 2009, no. 1, (2009), p. 143 (hereafter, "Epstein, 'Genetic Surveillance'").

[20] Henry T. Greely, Daniel P. Riordan, and Nanibaa' A. Garrison, et al., "Family Ties: The Use of DNA Offender Databases to Catch Offenders' Kin," *Journal of Law, Medicine and Ethics*, vol. 34, no. 2 (Summer 2006), p. 250 (hereafter, "Greely, Riordan, Garrison, et al., 'Family Ties'").

[21] Ibid.

[22] *Fundamentals of Forensic DNA Typing*, p. 270.

[23] Ibid., p. 271.

[24] U.S. Department of Justice, Federal Bureau of Investigation, *Quality Assurance Standards for DNA Databasing Laboratories*, Standard 15, http://www.fbi.gov/about-us/lab/codis/qas_databaselabs. U.S. Department of Justice, Federal Bureau of Investigation, *Quality Assurance Standards for Forensic DNA Testing Laboratories*, Standard 15, http://www.fbi.gov/about-us/lab/codis/qas_testlabs (hereafter "QAS").

[25] *Fundamentals of Forensic DNA Typing*, p. 271.

[26] Ibid.

[27] Ibid.

[28] U.S. Congress, House Committee on the Judiciary, Subcommittee on Crime, Terrorism, and Homeland Security, *Testimony of Jeffery S. Boschwitz, Ph.D.*, Hearing on "Rape Kit Backlogs: Failing the Test of Providing Justice to Sexual Assault Survivors", 111th Cong., 2nd sess., May 20, 2010, H.Hrg 111-115 (Washington: GPO, 2010), p. 81 (hereafter, "Testimony of Dr. Boschwitz")

casework in 2005, up from 19% in 2002.[29] All private laboratories that conduct DNA testing for public laboratories must be accredited, be audited annually, and adhere to the requirements of the QAS.[30] Public laboratories are required to conduct an initial site visit to each private laboratory it contracts with to conduct DNA analyses.[31] If the public laboratory signs a contract with a private laboratory that is longer than one year, the public laboratory must conduct an annual site visit.[32] Public laboratories are also required to review all outsourced DNA profiles generated by private laboratories.[33] The review by the public laboratory is in addition to the two reviews private laboratories are required to conduct per the QAS.

An offender or arrestee profile in a DNA database consists of 26 numbers representing each of the two alleles for the 13 STR loci, an agency identification number, a sample identification number, and an identifier for the analyst that entered the information.[34] However, most jurisdictions retain the DNA sample used to generate the profile placed in CODIS.[35] DNA samples are usually retained for quality assurance purposes, such as confirming a hit made using the NDIS, and it allows jurisdictions to retest the sample if new technology is developed in the future.[36] Privacy advocates are concerned that stored DNA samples include a wealth of genetic information that could be misused.[37] States and the federal government have sought to prevent the unauthorized use of DNA samples. Some states have criminal penalties in place for individuals who misuse DNA samples collected for law enforcement purposes.[38] Under current law, anyone who misuses a DNA sample collected under federal authority is subject to a fine of up to $250,000, or imprisonment for up to one year.[39]

The number of offender profiles included in the NDIS has increased as Congress has allowed states to include DNA profiles from a broader range of convicted offenders and persons arrested for certain crimes to be included in the database. States have also amended their DNA collection laws to reflect this expanded authority. As shown in **Table 1**, nearly 11 million new convicted offender and arrestee profiles have been added to NDIS over the past decade. This is in part because more forensic profiles have been added to the NDIS as state and local governments have started to work their way through backlogs of forensic casework. As also shown, over 400,000 new forensic profiles have been included in the NDIS since 2000. Data presented show that the expansion of the NDIS has mostly been driven by laboratories processing and entering offender profiles. The additional offender and forensic profiles have increased the number of investigate

---

[29] Matthew R. Durose, *Census of Publicly Funded Forensic Crime Laboratories, 2005*, U.S. Department of Justice, Office of Justice Programs, Bureau of Justice Statistics, NCJ 222181, Washington, DC, July 2008, p. 7, http://bjs.ojp.usdoj.gov/content/pub/pdf/cpffcl05.pdf (hereafter, *Census of Publicly Funded Forensic Crime Laboratories*).

[30] QAS, Standard 17.

[31] CODIS Fact Sheet.

[32] QAS, Standard 17.

[33] Ibid.

[34] *Fundamentals of Forensic DNA Typing*, p. 270.

[35] Ibid., p. 262.

[36] Ibid.

[37] Tania Simoncelli, "Dangerous Excursions: The Case Against Expanding Forensic DNA Databases to Innocent Persons," *Journal of Law, Medicine, and Ethics*, vol. 34, no. 2 (Summer 2006), p. 392 (hereafter "Simoncelli, 'Dangerous Excursions'").

[38] Simoncelli, "Dangerous Excursions," p. 392.

[39] 42 U.S.C. §14135e(c).

---

leads generated by DNA databases. Since 2000, the NDIS has aided in the investigation of nearly 175,000 crimes. Data in **Table 1** indicate that most matches occur between forensic and offender profiles stored in SDIS rather than the NDIS.

Table 1. Number of Profiles in the NDIS, Investigations Aided, and Hits Generated by Searches of NDIS

Year	Convicted Offender Profiles	Arrestee Profiles	Forensic Profiles	Investigations Aided	Forensic Hits	National Offender Hits (NDIS)	State Offender Hits (SDIS)	Total Offender Hits
2000	441,181	—	21,625	1,573	507	26	705	731
2002	1,247,163	—	46,177	6,670	1,832	638	4,394	5,032
2004	2,038,514	—	93,956	21,266	5,056	1,834	12,482	14,316
2006	3,977,435	54,313	160,582	45,364	9,493	4,397	30,138	34,535
2008	6,399,200	140,719	248,943	81,955	14,364	8,561	59,184	67,745
2010	8,564,705	668,849	351,951	130,317	21,983	15,724	97,772	113,496
2012a	9,761,083	1,139,065	436,937	174,680	28,993	20,698	132,517	153,215

Source: U.S. Department of Justice, Federal Bureau of Investigation, *CODIS Brochure.*

Notes: Amounts shown are cumulative starting with 2000. In the most recent *CODIS Brochure* the FBI published data on profiles in the NDIS for every other year starting with 2000. "Forensic hit" refers to cases where a match is made between two or more forensic profiles in the database. "Offender hit" refers to cases where an offender profile is matched to one or more forensic profile in the database.

a.   Through June 2012.

One limitation of the data in **Table 1** is that they do not describe how the investigations were aided, the outcomes of the investigations, or whether any of the hits solved the alleged crimes.[40] Database hits do not always generate a new investigative lead; investigators, if they have already identified a suspect and they know that the suspect's profile is already in the database, may enter a forensic profile into the database and wait for a hit to be returned before investigating further. In addition, not all hits generated by the DNA databases are probative; just because someone's DNA is found at a crime scene does not always mean that the person who left the DNA is the perpetrator. Also, it is possible that one forensic or offender hit might lead to several arrests or aid in multiple investigations. The data published by the FBI provide a measure of the output generated by the NDIS, but the "hits" and "investigations aided" metrics are poor indicators of whether DNA databases aided in resolving criminal investigations.[41] For example, the data provide no indication of whether the hits generated by the NDIS resulted in a conviction or how many investigations resulted in an arrest.

A study of database hits in San Francisco suggests that there is a need for more expansive data collection in order to properly to evaluate the effectiveness of DNA databases.[42] The study

---

[40] Frederick R. Bieber, "Turning Base Hits into Earned Runs: Improving the Effectiveness of Forensic DNA Data Bank Programs," *Journal of Law, Medicine and Ethics*, vol. 34, no. 2 (Summer 2006), p. 227.

[41] Ibid.

[42] Matthew Gabriel, Cherisse Boland, and Cydne Holt, "Beyond the Cold Hit: Measuring the Impact of the National DNA Data Bank on Public Safety at the City and County Level," *Journal of Law, Medicine and Ethics*, vol. 38, no. 2 (continued...)

measured the outcomes of 198 DNA database hits in cold cases[43] generated by the San Francisco Police Department Forensic Biology Unit between 2001 and 2006. The researchers report that 90% of the cold hits were probative and provided investigators with substantive leads.[44] Probative hits led to judicial resolution (i.e., conviction, guilty plea, or parole revocation) 40% of the time.[45] Another 28% of the cases involving probative hits were either awaiting jury trial or the investigation was ongoing at the time the article was written. The researchers note that they found that nearly 70% of the probative hits could result in some form of judicial resolution. There were varying rates of success for database hits for different types of offenses. Nearly 9 in 10 probative hits in homicide and burglary cases either reached judicial resolution or could be resolved. However, judicial resolution or potential resolution was lower for sex offenses (approximately 1 in 2). In nearly half of the cases where a probative hit was made for a sex offense, either the prosecutor (17%) or the victim (31%) declined to move the case forward.[46]

Collection of DNA Samples from State Offenders

Since the late 1990s, state laws have changed to require a greater number of offenders, and in some cases arrestees, to submit a DNA sample for analysis and inclusion in states' databases. When the NDIS was first started in 1998, most states only collected DNA samples from individuals convicted of violent felonies and felony sexual offenses. Over the years, more states passed laws requiring collection of DNA samples from a broader range of offenders. In 1999, only five states collected DNA samples from all convicted felons.[47] By 2004, the number of states that collected DNA samples from all convicted felons increased to 37, and four years later, 47 states collected DNA samples from all convicted felons.[48] Currently, all states require all convicted felons to submit a DNA sample and 37 states require individuals convicted of misdemeanor sexual offenses to submit a DNA sample (see **Appendix**).[49] Moreover, 34 states collect DNA samples from juveniles adjudicated for certain offenses and all states collect DNA samples from offenders on probation.[50] More recently, some states have enacted laws to require individuals *arrested* (not just convicted) for certain offenses to provide a DNA sample for analysis and inclusion in the NDIS. Currently, 25 states require individuals arrested for murder and sexual offenses to provide a DNA sample.[51] Of these states, 22 require individuals arrested

---

(...continued)

(Summer 2010), pp. 396-411.

[43] Ibid., p. 397. "Cold cases" were defined as crimes where the investigation has not generated a named suspect(s) through traditional methods of police investigation (e.g., interviewing witnesses, identification through non-DNA physical evidence left at the crime scene, or tips from confidential informants).

[44] Ibid., p. 398.

[45] Ibid., p. 400.

[46] Ibid.

[47] *Fundamentals of Forensic DNA Typing*, p. 278.

[48] Ibid.

[49] Gordon Thomas Honeywell, Governmental Affairs, *State DNA Database Laws, Qualifying Offenses*, http://www.dnaresource.com/documents/statequalifyingoffenses2011.pdf.

[50] Ibid.

[51] Ibid.

for burglary to submit a DNA sample.[52] More than half (13) of the 25 states require individuals arrested for all felony offenses to submit a DNA sample.[53]

DNA Backlog

Delays in processing DNA evidence can result in delays in apprehending or prosecuting violent or serial offenders or it can result in wrongfully convicted individuals serving time in prison for crimes they did not commit. In addition, persistent backlogs can result in crime laboratories prioritizing DNA analysis for violent offenses, such as homicide or sexual assault, over other offenses, such as property crimes, or it can result in law enforcement agencies establishing policies stating that biological evidence is not to be collected for minor offenses.[54] Not analyzing or collecting DNA samples for minor offenses could prevent law enforcement from apprehending offenders before they commit more serious crimes. Data indicate that many violent offenders start off with committing property crimes.[55]

Forensic Casework

In a February 2011 report, the National Institute of Justice (NIJ) published estimates of the forensic casework backlogs in state and local laboratories in 2005, 2007, 2008, and 2009 (presented in **Figure 1**).[56] Different methodologies used to collect the data and survey response rates differed slightly, but the data show a pattern: the backlog of forensic casework continues to increase as the demand for forensic DNA casework continues to outpace the crime laboratory capacity to conduct such analyses.[57] It is important to remember that data presented in **Figure 1** present a national picture of the forensic DNA backlog; it is likely that some crime laboratories have little or no backlog, while other laboratories have significant backlogs.[58] Data also show that the backlog of forensic casework is not the result of a glut of old samples awaiting analysis;

---

[52] Ibid.

[53] Ibid.

[54] Edwin Zedlewski and Mary B. Murphy, "DNA Analysis for 'Minor' Crimes: A Major Benefit for Law Enforcement," *NIJ Journal*, vol. 253 (January 2006) (hereafter, "DNA Analysis for 'Minor' Crimes").

[55] Data from BJS show that approximately 1 in 5 property offenders released from prison in 1994 were rearrested for a violent crime with three years. Patrick A. Langan and David J. Levin, *Recidivism of Prisoners Released in 1994*, U.S. Department of Justice, Office of Justice Programs, Bureau of Justice Statistics, NCJ 193427, Washington, DC, June 2002, p. 9, http://bjs.ojp.usdoj.gov/content/pub/pdf/rpr94.pdf. In addition, a study of DNA databases hits in Florida show that 52% of hits for homicide and sexual assault cases matched offenders who had prior convictions for burglary. DNA Analysis for "Minor" Crimes.

[56] NIJ defines a backlogged case as a case that has not been analyzed within 30 days of being submitted to the laboratory. Mark Nelson, *Making Sense of DNA Backlogs—Myths vs. Reality*, U.S. Department of Justice, Office of Justice Programs, National Institute of Justice, NCJ 323197, Washington, DC, February 2011, p. 3, http://www.ncjrs.gov/pdffiles1/nij/232197.pdf (hereafter, *Making Sense of DNA Backlogs—Myths vs. Reality*).

[57] Backlog data for 2005 were collected as a part of the Bureau of Justice Statistic's Census of Publicly Funded Forensic Crime Laboratories (see Matthew R. Durose, *Census of Publicly Funded Forensic Crime Laboratories, 2005*, NCJ 222181, July 2008, http://bjs.ojp.usdoj.gov/content/pub/pdf/cpffcl05.pdf). Data for 2007 were collected as a part of a NIJ funded study of DNA backlogs (see Lisa Hurst and Kevin Lothridge, "2007 DNA Evidence and Offender Measurement Analysis: DNA Backlogs, Capacity and Funding," NCJ 230328, January 2010, http://www.ncjrs.gov/pdffiles1/nij/grants/230328.pdf). Data for 2008 were reported by applicants for NIJ's FY2009 DNA Backlog Reduction Program grant solicitation. Data for 2009 were reported by applicants for NIJ's FY2010 DNA Backlog Reduction Program. Ibid., p. 3.

[58] Ibid., p. 4.

rather, the forensic casework backlog is mostly driven by increasing demand for DNA analysis in new cases. NIJ reports that the growing demand for DNA analysis is increasing for many reasons, including

- a growing awareness of the potential of DNA evidence to solve cases;

- more DNA samples are being collected from property crimes;

- advances in DNA technology allow tests to be conducted on smaller samples of DNA;

- more DNA testing in old, unsolved cases where the evidence was collected before DNA testing became widespread; and

- post-conviction DNA testing.[59]

Another contributing factor to the forensic casework backlog is the labor-intensive nature of processing forensic casework. NIJ reports that processing forensic evidence is time-consuming because the evidence must be screened to determine if, and what kind of, biological materials are present before DNA testing can begin.[60]

Figure 1. DNA Forensic Casework: Supply, Demands, Backlogs

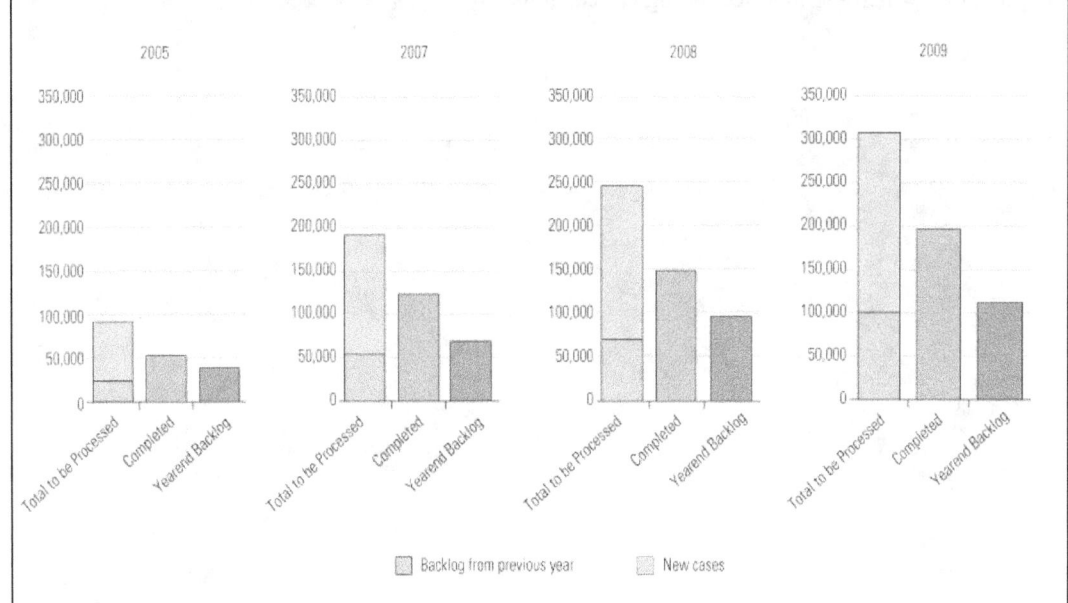

Source: CRS reproduction of a figure from the U.S. Department of Justice, Office of Justice Programs, National Institute of Justice, "Making Sense of DNA Backlogs—Myths vs. Reality," p. 3.

Notes: Backlog data for 2005 were collected as a part of the Bureau of Justice Statistic's 2005 Census of Publicly Funded Forensic Crime Laboratories. Data for 2007 were collected as a part of a NIJ-funded study of DNA backlogs. Data for 2008 and 2009 were reported by applicants for NIJ's FY2009 and FY2010 DNA Backlog Reduction Program grant solicitations. Data are not available for 2006. Data for 2009 is the most recent available.

---

[59] Ibid.

[60] Ibid., p. 1.

Convicted Offender and Arrestee Samples

In addition to the backlog of forensic casework, there is a backlog in the processing of samples collected from convicted offenders and arrestees. Backlogs of convicted offender and arrestee samples means that there are fewer DNA profiles in CODIS to match forensic profiles to, and this could result in a delay in identifying suspects in cases where DNA evidence was collected. Data collected by NIJ show that submission of new DNA samples from convicted offenders and arrestees increased between 2007 and 2009 (see **Figure 2**).[61] At the same time, the total number of convicted offender and arrestee samples analyzed decreased between 2007 and 2008, but the number of samples analyzed remained at approximately 1 million in both 2008 and 2009.[62] Therefore, the increased backlog of convicted offender and arrestee samples between 2008 and 2009 was the result of states collecting more offender samples, especially from arrestees, while the ability to analyze those samples remained flat.

Data indicate that there are more convicted offender and arrestee DNA samples for laboratories to process compared to forensic samples; NIJ notes, however, that offender and arrestee samples are easier and faster to analyze because they are collected on a standard, consistent medium.[63] The standardized collection method makes it possible to use automated analysis on robotic platforms that can process approximately 96 samples and controls simultaneously.[64] This suggests that laboratories might be better able to process the backlog of convicted offender and arrestee samples if they increase their technological capacity.

---

[61] Ibid., p. 7.

[62] Ibid., p. 8.

[63] Ibid., p. 2.

[64] Ibid.

Figure 2. Convicted Offender and Arrestee Backlog Trends, 2007-2009

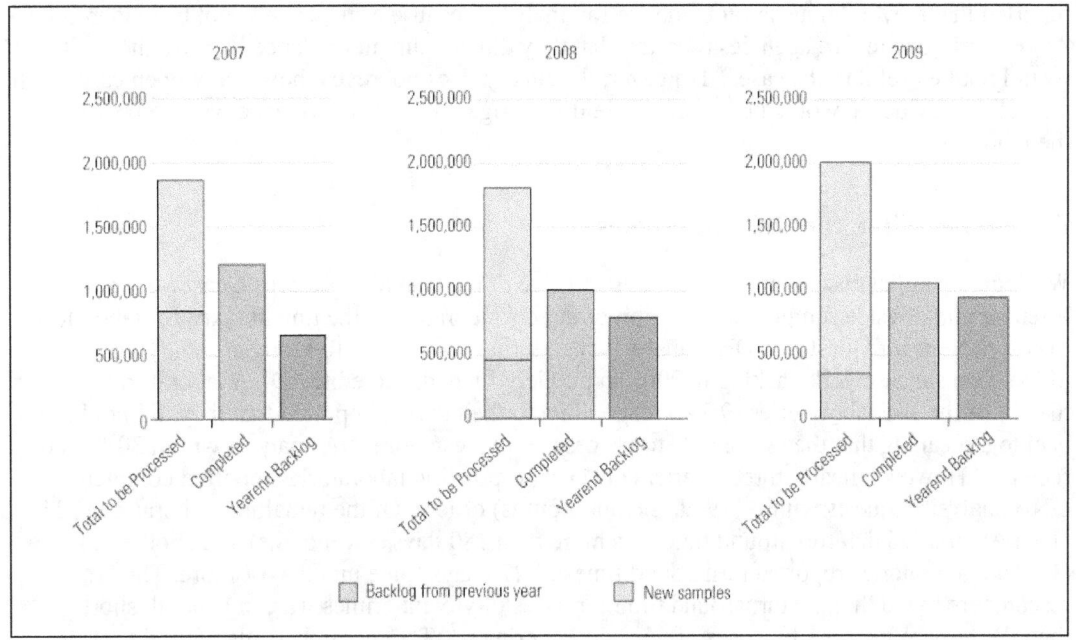

Source: U.S. Department of Justice, Office of Justice Programs, National Institute of Justice, "Making Sense of DNA Backlogs—Myths vs. Reality," p. 7.

Notes: Data for 2007 were collected as a part of a NIJ-funded study of DNA backlogs. Data for 2008 and 2009 were reported by applicants for NIJ's FY2009 and FY2010 DNA Backlog Reduction Program grant solicitations. Data for 2009 is the most recent available.

Evidence in the Possession of Law Enforcement

One limitation to the backlog data discussed above is that they only include samples in the possession of crime laboratories. Samples from evidence still in the possession of law enforcement agencies and not yet transferred to laboratories are not counted as a part of the backlog. While there is no current count of the total amount of unanalyzed evidence in the possession of law enforcement agencies, one group of researchers that surveyed over 2,000 law enforcement agencies in 2007 found that law enforcement agencies had forensic evidence that had not been submitted to a crime laboratory for analysis in 14% of all unsolved homicide cases and 18% of unsolved rape cases.[65] The researchers estimated that nearly 40% of unanalyzed murder and rape cases contained DNA evidence.[66] The results of the survey indicate that there are many reasons why law enforcement agencies chose not to submit evidence for analysis, including that subsequent investigation may have shown that the evidence would not be probative; charges against an alleged perpetrator may have been dropped; or the suspect may have pled guilty.[67] However, data collected by the researchers also suggest that law enforcement agencies may not fully understand the potential value forensic evidence can have in generating leads in cases where

---

[65] Kevin J. Strom, Jeri Ropero-Miller, and Shelton Jones, et al., *The 2007 Survey of Law Enforcement Forensic Evidence Processing*, U.S. Department of Justice, Office of Justice Programs, National Institute of Justice, Washington, DC, October 2009, pp. 3-2, http://www.ncjrs.gov/pdffiles1/nij/grants/228415.pdf.

[66] Ibid.

[67] Ibid., p. 3-7.

---

they have not identified a suspect. Nearly half of the responding law enforcement agencies reported that they did not submit evidence for analysis because a suspect had not been identified. Also, nearly one in five agencies reported that they did not submit evidence because they felt it would not be useful to the case.[68] However, the survey does not reveal how many open cases with unanalyzed evidence would be solved or yield investigative leads if evidence were to be sent to the laboratory.

Processing Time for DNA Analyses

While many policymakers are interested in the size of the backlog of forensic casework and offender and arrestee samples, another important consideration is the time it takes for laboratories to complete new requests for DNA analysis (i.e., turnaround time). Researchers studying the size of the forensic casework backlog in 2007 in publicly funded, accredited DNA laboratories found that 14 of the 145 laboratories (9.7%) responding to their survey reported that they did not have a backlog, meaning that they were able to process all requests for DNA analysis within 30 days of receipt.[69] However, nearly three-quarters (111) of responding laboratories reported completing DNA analysis requests within 119 days (four months) or less. Of the remaining laboratories, 24 (16.6%) reported that turnaround time was more than 180 days (six months) and another 20 (13.8%) laboratories reported turnaround times of 270 days (nine months) or more. The researchers found that the turnaround time for cases of violent crimes was, in general, shorter than the turnaround time for cases of non-violent crimes.[70] The researchers also found that the turnaround time for analysis of offender and arrestee samples tended to be shorter than the turnaround time for forensic casework. Approximately 30% of responding laboratories reported having turnaround times of 30 days or less for offender and arrestee samples.[71] Approximately half of all responding laboratories reported processing offender and arrestee samples within 90 days of receipt. However, one-quarter of laboratories reported turnaround times of more than 270 days (nine months) for these samples.[72]

Sexual Assault Evidence Collection Kits

Recently, the backlog of sexual assault evidence collections kits—also referred to as "rape kits"—has been the focus of a congressional hearing and several pieces of legislation.[73] While there have

---

[68] Ibid., p. 3-6.

[69] Lisa Hurst and Kevin Lothridge, *2007 DNA Evidence and Offender Analysis Measurement: DNA Backlogs, Capacity and Funding*, Final Report to National Institute of Justice Grant 2006-MU-BX-K002, Washington, DC, January 2010, p. 8, http://www.ncjrs.gov/pdffiles1/nij/grants/230328.pdf (hereafter, *2007 DNA Evidence and Offender Analysis Measurement*).

[70] Ibid.

[71] Ibid., p. 12.

[72] Ibid.

[73] In the 111th Congress, the House Subcommittee on Crime, Terrorism, and Homeland Security held a hearing on sexual assault evidence collection kit backlogs. See U.S. Congress, House Committee on the Judiciary, Subcommittee on Crime, Terrorism, and Homeland Security, Hearing on "Rape Kit Backlogs: Failing the Test of Providing Justice to Sexual Assault Survivors," 111th Cong., 2nd sess., May 20, 2010, H.Hrg 111-115 (Washington: GPO, 2010). Also, several pieces of legislation in the 111th Congress would have, among other things, provided funding for processing backlogged sexual assault evidence collection kits, made eligibility for funding under certain Department of Justice (DOJ) grant programs contingent on eliminating the backlog of sexual assault evidence collection kits, or provided for the collection of data on the backlog of kits. See H.R. 4114, S. 2736, H.R. 5640, H.R. 6085, S. 3842, and H.R. 6214 in the 111th Congress and S. 250, S. 254, S. 3250, H.R. 1523, and H.R. 6628 in the 112th Congress.

---

been several estimates of the backlog in some cities,[74] NIJ reports that currently there is no comprehensive data on the number of unanalyzed sexual assault evidence kits in the United States.[75] NIJ reports that it is currently funding research to better understand why some sexual assault evidence collection kits are not submitted to a crime laboratory for analysis.[76] The backlog of sexual assault evidence collection kits has raised concerns that additional victimizations could have been prevented had the evidence from any given kit been tested and the perpetrator apprehended in a timely manner.[77]

Sexual assault evidence collection kits are collections of tools used by a nurse examiner or another trained professional to collect evidence during a forensic medical exam conducted after someone has reported a sexual assault and consents to the exam.[78] Many jurisdictions have developed their own sexual assault evidence collection kits, or they purchase them from a commercial vendor. As such, the content of a kit can vary from jurisdiction to jurisdiction.[79] In general, sexual assault evidence collection kits include (1) instructions; (2) bags, sheets, and envelopes for evidence collection; (3) swabs for collecting fluids or secretions that could contain the perpetrator's DNA; (4) a comb for collecting hair samples; (5) blood collection devices; and (6) documentation forms.[80] An exam involves collecting a complete medical history from the victim and completing a full-body physical examination.[81] This may include

- collecting blood, urine, hair, and other body secretion samples;

- photo documentation of any injuries sustained during the assault;

- collecting the victim's clothing, especially undergarments; and

- collecting any possible physical evidence that may have transferred onto the victim from the crime scene.[82]

In addition to jurisdictional differences in the content of sexual assault evidence collection kits, procedures for analyzing the evidence collected using the kit can vary from jurisdiction to jurisdiction. In some jurisdictions, all sexual assault evidence collection kits are forwarded to a

---

[74] CBS News conducted a five month investigation into the backlog of sexual assault evidence collection kits. The investigation collected data on the number of backlogged kits in 24 cities and states. CBS News reports that there are more than 20,000 sexual assault evidence collection kits that were never sent to crime laboratories and another 6,000 kits from cases that are under active investigation, but are still waiting to be tested. The results of CBS News' investigation are available online at http://www.cbsnews.com/stories/2009/11/10/cbsnews_investigates/main5605770.shtml?tag=contentMain;contentBody.

[75] Nancy Ritter, "Solving the Problem of Untested Evidence in Sexual Assaults," *NIJ Journal*, no. 267 (Winter 2010), p. 18.

[76] Ibid., p. 19.

[77] Armen Keteyian, "Untested Rape Kits Lead to More Crimes," *CBS News*, November 10, 2009, http://www.cbsnews.com/stories/2009/11/10/cbsnews_investigates/main5603492.shtml.

[78] Rape, Abuse and Incest National Network (RAINN), *What is a Rape Kit*, http://www.rainn.org/get-information/sexual-assault-recovery/rape-kit (hereafter, *What is a Rape Kit*).

[79] U.S. Department of Justice, Office on Violence Against Women, *A National Protocol for Sexual Assault Medical Forensic Examinations*, NCJ 206554, September 2004, p. 65, http://www.ncjrs.gov/pdffiles1/ovw/206554.pdf (hereafter, *A National Protocol for Sexual Assault Medical Forensic Examinations*).

[80] *What is a Rape Kit*.

[81] Ibid.

[82] Ibid.

crime laboratory for analysis.[83] In other jurisdictions, it may be months or even years before the kit is tested, if at all.[84] Some law enforcement agencies might not submit sexual assault evidence collection kits to crime laboratories for various reasons: the identity of the perpetrator was not in question from the beginning of the investigation, detectives identified the suspect through other evidence not included in the kit, or the victim chooses not to proceed with the case.[85] Also, some law enforcement agencies might have a problem working through their backlog of old kits because crime laboratories are operating at full capacity analyzing DNA evidence collected from current cases.[86]

Investigation of Leads Generated from Database Hits

While reducing casework backlogs can help generate new leads in cases without suspects (so-called "cold cases"), law enforcement agencies have to devote time to investigating the leads that result from DNA database matches. Data from a 2009 survey of 235 law enforcement agencies suggest that law enforcement agencies, particularly small agencies, might not have the resources to fully investigate new leads. The survey found that 37% of agencies surveyed had designated "cold case units" (i.e., groups of investigators who are responsible for leads generated from a match between an offender and forensic profile in either the SDIS or the NDIS).[87] In addition, the larger the agency (as measured by the number of sworn officers) the more likely they were to have such a unit. Over two-thirds of law enforcement agencies with 1,000 or more sworn officers reported having a cold case unit.[88] However, less than half of law enforcement agencies with 379-999 sworn officers reported having this unit, and less than 20% of agencies with 378 or fewer sworn officers reported having such a unit.[89] Even if an agency reported having a cold case unit, the unit was typically small. Three-quarters of law enforcement agencies with cold case units reported that three or fewer staff members were assigned to the unit.[90] Law enforcement agencies that did not have cold case units reported that leads generated from DNA database hits were investigated when resources were available, which usually meant that investigators were paid overtime to follow-up on the new leads.[91] Data suggest that law enforcement agencies would expand cold case units if they had the resources. Surveyed law enforcement agencies were asked to identify, based on their agency's experiences, the resources they needed for DNA-related work.

---

[83] Angela Wu, "Will Rape Kit Testing Laws Help Clear Cases?," *Newsweek*, July 27, 2010, http://www.newsweek.com/2010/07/27/will-rape-kit-testing-laws-help-clear-cases.html (hereafter, "Will Rape Kit Testing Laws Help Clear Cases?").

[84] Human Rights Watch, *Testing Justice: The Rape Kit Backlog in Los Angeles City and County*, 1-56432-461-3, New York, NY, March 2009, p. 22, http://www.hrw.org/node/81826.

[85] U.S. Department of Justice, Office of Justice Programs, National Institute of Justice, *Untested Sexual Assault Evidence in Law Enforcement Custody*, http://www.nij.gov/topics/forensics/lab-operations/evidence-backlogs/law-enforcement-sexual-assault.htm.

[86] Department of Justice, Office on Violence Against Women, *Eliminating the Rape Kit Backlog: A Roundtable to Explore a Victim-centered Approach*, Washington , DC, May 10, 2010, p. 15, http://www.ovw.usdoj.gov/docs/rape-kit-roundtable-summary-10262010.pdf.

[87] Dan Cantillon, Kathy Kopiec, and Heather Clawson, *Evaluation of the Impact of the Forensic Casework DNA Backlog Reduction Program*, ICF International, Fairfax, VA, February 2009, p. 10, http://www.ncjrs.gov/pdffiles1/nij/grants/225803.pdf (hereafter, *Evaluation of the Impact of the Forensic Casework DNA Backlog Reduction Program*").

[88] Ibid., p. 11.

[89] Ibid.

[90] Ibid., p. 10.

[91] Ibid., p. 11.

Two-thirds identified cold case unit staffing (both for staffing cold case units or paying overtime if the agency did not have a cold case unit) as a need.[92]

Partial Match Searching

Crime laboratories can use three levels of stringency—high, moderate, and low—when using CODIS to search for matches between an offender or arrestee and forensic profiles. Searches with high stringency require a match between all 26 alleles,[93] which, as discussed above, indicates that it is highly probable that the identified offender or arrestee was the source of the forensic sample. A moderate stringency search requires all available alleles to match, but the profiles can contain a different number of alleles.[94] Moderate stringency searches can be used to search for matches when the forensic profile contains a mixture of DNA from two or more sources, hence there might be more than two alleles at some loci. Low stringency searches require one allele at each loci to match.[95] Low stringency searches are sometimes required because a degraded sample might not have alleles at all loci.[96]

Crime laboratories can use low stringency searches to make partial matches between and offender or arrestee and forensic profiles. Partial match searching can be used for familial searching, which involves using DNA from known individuals in a database to identify relatives of those individuals as potential suspects in other crimes.[97] There is some debate about whether partial match searching is the same as familial searching. In some states, crime laboratories can release information on partial matches that result from a regular search of the SDIS or NDIS, but they do not consider these partial matches to be familial searches because they were not the result of a *deliberate* search of the database for partial matches between an offender or arrestee and forensic profiles.[98] Others argue that even if the partial match was not the result of a deliberate search of the database, it is still a familial search because it could implicate the relative of someone with a profile in the database.[99] Research indicates that there is a lack of transparency when it comes to policies regarding partial matches. In most cases where a state reports the results of partial matches, it is done without explicit statutory authorization, and in many instances the policy is unwritten or it is not available to the public.[100]

Familial searching is possible because of the way humans inherit genes. Close relatives—especially parents, children, and siblings—who are genetically related are more likely to share

---

[92] Ibid., p. 14.

[93] *Fundamentals of Forensic DNA Typing*, p. 275.

[94] Ibid.

[95] Ibid.

[96] The FBI permits forensic profiles with 10 of the 13 CODIS loci to be uploaded into the NDIS for searching against the offender and arrestee indexes. CODIS Fact Sheet.

[97] David Lazer, *Searching the Family Tree for Suspects: Ethical and Implementation Issues in the Familial Searching of DNA Databases*, A. Alfred Taubman Center for State and Local Government, Cambridge, MA, March 2008, p. 1, http://www.hks.harvard.edu/var/ezp_site/storage/fckeditor/file/pdfs/centers-programs/centers/taubman/policybriefs/lazer_final.pdf (hereafter, Lazer, *Searching the Family Tree for Suspects*).

[98] Natalie Ram, *DNA Confidential: State Law Enforcement Policies for Genetic Databases Lack Transparency*, Science Progress, October 2009, p. 2, http://www.scienceprogress.org/2009/11/dna-confidential/.

[99] Ibid., p. 1.

[100] Ibid., p. 3.

---

alleles used for identification in CODIS than two people who are not closely related.[101] Two unrelated people usually only share a few CODIS alleles, but a parent and his or her child must share no fewer than 13 alleles since children inherit half of their genes from each parent.[102] Parents and children will most likely share between 14 and 16 alleles.[103] It is possible that two siblings will share between 0 and 26 alleles, but on average they will share 16.7 alleles.[104] Familial searching can be conducted by using low stringency searching, but low stringency searches can result in hundreds or even thousands of partial matches, none of which might actually represent a biological relationship. The probability that two unrelated people will share more than 13 alleles with at least one match at each of the 13 loci is about 1 in 2,000.[105] While this probability is low, there are over 8.6 million offender profiles in the NDIS, meaning that a low stringency search for a common genotype could generate thousands of partial matches.

The FBI has been reluctant to allow the NDIS to be used for familial searching without explicit legislative approval,[106] but in July 2006 the FBI issued a policy that permits states, at their discretion, to share identification information with other states in the event that a search of the NDIS turns up a partial match.[107] While the FBI's policy might seem to be at odds with the bureau's reluctance to allow the NDIS to be used for familial searching, a closer review of the FBI's definition of "familial searching" shows how the FBI could allow states to share partial match information without contradicting its stance on familial searching. The FBI defines familial searching "as a 'second deliberate search ... to identify close biological relatives of the perpetrator in the known offender database,' used only after an initial search of the database turns up no candidate matches."[108] The FBI's current policy allows states to share any partial matches; they do not have to be the result of a deliberate search for relatives of individuals with a profile in the NDIS. The FBI's policy means that states have the final say over whether to release identifying information in the case of partial matches.

Post-conviction DNA Testing

In addition to aiding law enforcement in criminal investigations, DNA testing also provides wrongfully convicted prisoners with an avenue to have their convictions overturned. As of April 2011, the Innocence Project reports that 268 prisoners have been exonerated through post-conviction DNA testing.[109] Currently, all states except Massachusetts and Oklahoma have enacted post-conviction DNA testing statutes.[110] However, some states limit who can apply for post-

---

[101] Greely, Riordan, Garrison, et al., "Family Ties," p. 251.

[102] Ibid., p. 252.

[103] Ibid.

[104] Ibid., p. 253.

[105] Ibid., p. 252.

[106] Ellen Nakashima, "From DNA of Family, a Tool to Make Arrests," *The Washington Post*, April 21, 2008.

[107] The FBI defines a "partial match" as a match between two single source profiles (i.e., offender profiles and forensic profiles that contain DNA from one perpetrator) having at least one allele in common at each locus. U.S. Department of Justice, Federal Bureau of Investigation, "Interim Plan for the Release of Information In the Event of a 'Partial Match' at NDIS," Bulletin #BT072006, July 20, 2006, http://www.bioforensics.com/conference08/Familial_Searches/CODIS_Bulletin.pdf.

[108] Sonia M. Suter, "All in the Family: Privacy and DNA Familial Searching," *Harvard Journal of Law and Technology*, vol. 23, no. 2 (Spring 2010), p. 324 (hereafter, Suter, "All in the Family").

[109] The Innocence Project, http://www.innocenceproject.org/.

[110] Ala. Code §15-18-200; Alaska Stat. §§12.73.010 through 12.73.090; Ariz. Rev. Stat. Ann. §13-4240; Ark. Stat. (continued...)

conviction DNA testing. In some states, only individuals sentenced to death or convicted for certain offenses (usually violent offenses) can apply for post-conviction DNA testing. In nearly half the states (24), anyone convicted of a *felony* is eligible to apply for post-conviction DNA testing. However, some states (20) allow *anyone* convicted of a crime to apply for post-conviction DNA testing.

While nearly all states have laws allowing certain individuals access to post-conviction DNA testing, access to testing can be rendered moot if evidence is not preserved or if it is preserved in a manner where there is a chance for it to be contaminated or degraded. Currently, 37 states have statutes that provide for the preservation of evidence after someone is convicted.[111] However, each state has its own standard regarding whether law enforcement agencies are required to retain biological evidence after someone has been convicted of a crime, how long agencies are required to retain evidence, and if there are any requirements for the conditions in which evidence must be stored.

Current Federal Statutory Law

While state law dictates whose profiles will be included in each state's DNA database, federal law provides for the collection of DNA samples from certain federal offenders for analysis and inclusion in the NDIS. Federal law also dictates which profiles included in SDIS can be uploaded into the NDIS. Federal law also states that agencies participating in the NDIS must meet certain specified standards. In addition, federal law provides for post-conviction DNA testing for federal offenders. The following section summarizes current federal law as it pertains to DNA used in a criminal justice capacity.

(...continued)

Ann. §§16-112-201 through 16-112-208; Cal. Penal Code §1405; Colo. Rev. Stat §§18-1-411 through 18-1-416; Conn. Gen. Stat. §54-102-kk; Del. Code Ann. Tit. 11 §4504; Fla. Stat. §§925.11 and 925.12; Ga. Code §5-5-41; Hawaii Rev. Stat. §§844D-121 through 844D-133; Idaho Code §§19-4901 through 19-4911; Ill. Rev. Stat. Ch. 725, §5/116-3; Ind. Code §§35-38-7-1 through 35-38-7-13 and 35-38-7-17 through 35-38-7-19; Iowa Code §81.10; Kan. Stat. Ann. §21-2512; Ky. Rev. Stat. §§422.285 through 422.287; La. Code. Crim. Pro. §926.1; Me. Rev. Stat. Ann. Tit. 15 §§2136 through 2138; Md. Crim. Proc. Code Ann. §8-201; Mich. Comp. Laws §770.16; Minn. Stat. §§590.01 through 590.06; Miss. Code Ann. §99-39-5; Mo. Rev. Stat §547.035; Mont. Code Ann. §46-21-110; Neb. Rev. Stat §§29-2101 and 29-4117 through 29-4124; Nev. Rev. Stat. §176.0918; N.H. Rev. Stat. Ann §§651-D:1 through 651-D:4; N.J. Rev. Stat. §2A:84A-32a; N.M. Stat. Ann §31-1A-2; N.Y. Crim. Pro. Law §440.30; N.C. Gen. Stat. §§15A-269 through 15A-270.1; N.D. Cent. Code §29-32.1-15; Ohio Rev. Code Ann. §§2953.71 through 2953.83; Or. Rev. Stat. §§138.690 through 138.698; Pa. Cons. Stat. Tit. 42, §9543.1; R.I. Gen. Laws §§10-9.1-11 and 10-9.1-12; S.C. Code Ann. §§17-28-10 through 17-28-120; S.D. Codified Laws Ann. §§23-5B-1 through 23-5B-17; Tenn. Code Ann. §§40-30-301 through 40-30-313; Tex. Crim. Proc. Code Ann. §§64.01 through 64.05; Utah Code Ann. §§78B-9-301 through 78B-9-304; Vt. Stat. Ann. Tit. §§5561 through 5577; Va. Code §19.2-371.1; Wash. Rev. Code Ann. §10.73.170; W. Va. Code §15-2B-14; Wis. Stat. §974.07; and Wyo. Stat. §§7-12-302 through 7-12-315.

[111] Alaska Stat. §12.73.200; Ariz. Rev. Stat. Ann. §13-4221; Ark. Stat. Ann. §12-12-104; Cal. Penal Code §1417.9; Colo. Rev. Stat §§18-1-1101 through 18-1-1108; Conn. Gen. Stat. §54-102-jj; Fla. Stat. §925.11; Ga. Code §17-5-56; Hawaii Rev. Stat. §844D-126; Ill. Rev. Stat. Ch. 725, §5/116-4; Ind. Code §35-38-7-14; Iowa Code §81.10; Ky. Rev. Stat. §422.285; La. Code. Crim. Pro. §926.1; Md. Crim. Proc. Code Ann. §8-201; Mich. Comp. Laws §770.16; Minn. Stat. §590.10; Miss. Code Ann. §99-49-1; Mo. Rev. Stat §650.056; Mont. Code Ann. §46-21-111; Neb. Rev. Stat §29-4125; Nev. Rev. Stat. §176.0912; N.H. Rev. Stat. Ann §651-D:3; N.M. Stat. Ann §31-1A-2; N.C. Gen. Stat. §15A-268; Ohio Rev. Code Ann. §2953.81; R.I. Gen. Laws §10-9.1-11; S.C. Code Ann. §17-28-70; S.D. Codified Laws Ann. §23-5B-5; Tenn. Code Ann. §40-30-309; Tex. Gov. Code Ann. §411.052 and Tex. Crim. Proc. Code Ann. §38.43; Va. Code §19.2-270.4:1; Wash. Rev. Code Ann. §10.73.170; Wis. Stat. §968.205; and Wyo. Stat. §7-12-304.

Quality Assurance and Proficiency Testing Standards

Under current law,[112] the FBI is required to issue (and revise from time to time) Quality Assurance Standards (QAS), including standards for testing the proficiency of forensic laboratories and forensic analysts, in conducting DNA analyses.[113] By law, the QAS must specify the criteria for quality assurance and proficiency tests to be applied to the various types of DNA analyses conducted by forensic laboratories.[114] In addition, the QAS must include a system for grading proficiency testing performance to determine whether a laboratory is performing acceptably.[115] Under current law, FBI personnel who perform DNA analyses must undergo semiannual external proficiency testing by a DNA proficiency testing program that meets the standards set in the QAS.[116]

According to the FBI, the QAS describe the minimum standards for a laboratory's quality assurance program if performing forensic DNA analysis.[117] The minimum standards cover the following areas: organization, personnel, facilities, evidence or sample control, validation, analytical procedures, equipment calibration and maintenance, reports, review, proficiency testing, corrective action, audits, safety, and outsourcing.[118]

Index to Facilitate Law Enforcement Exchange of DNA Identification Information

The Violent Crime Control and Law Enforcement Act of 1994 (P.L. 103-322) authorized the FBI to establish an index of DNA profiles (i.e., NDIS). Under current law,[119] the NDIS can contain the DNA profiles of samples

- taken from individuals convicted of or charged with a crime, or collected under applicable legal authorities (e.g., people arrested for crimes), except for DNA samples that are voluntarily submitted solely for elimination purposes;

- recovered from crime scenes;

- recovered from unidentified human remains; and

- voluntarily contributed from relatives of missing persons.[120]

---

[112] 42 U.S.C. §14131(a)(2).

[113] The most recent QAS took effect on July 1, 2009.

[114] 42 U.S.C. §14131(a)(3).

[115] Ibid.

[116] 42 U.S.C. §14133(a)(1)(A).

[117] CODIS Fact Sheet.

[118] Ibid.

[119] 42 U.S.C. §14132(a).

[120] Under the Violent Crime Control and Law Enforcement Act of 1994 (P.L. 103-322), the NDIS was only to include analyses of DNA samples collected from (1) individuals convicted of crimes, (2) crime scenes, and (3) unidentified human remains. The Justice for All Act of 2004 (P.L. 108-405) amended the authorizing legislation for the NDIS to allow analyses of DNA samples collected from persons who have been charged in an indictment or information with a crime and other persons whose DNA samples are collected under applicable legal authorities to be included in the NDIS, provided that profiles from arrestees who have not been charged with a crime and samples that are voluntarily submitted solely for elimination purposes are not included in the NDIS. The Violence Against Women and Department (continued...)

The NDIS can only include DNA profiles

- based on analyses performed by or on behalf of a criminal justice agency or the Department of Defense (DOD) in accordance with available standards that satisfy or exceed the FBI's published QAS;

- that are prepared by laboratories that (1) have been accredited by a nonprofit professional organization of persons actively involved in forensic science and nationally recognized within the forensic science community, and (2) undergo external audits, not less than once every other year, that demonstrate compliance with the FBI's QAS;[121] and

- that are maintained by federal, state, and local criminal justice agencies or the DOD pursuant to rules that allow the disclosure of profiles only to other criminal justice agencies for identification purposes, judicial proceedings, criminal defense purposes, and, if personally identifiable information is removed, for research and quality control purposes.[122]

Under current law, the FBI is required to expunge the DNA profile of an individual who had a DNA profile entered into the NDIS on the basis of being convicted for a qualifying federal offense (see below) if the individual provides a certified copy of a final court order showing that the conviction was overturned.[123] Also, the FBI is required to expunge the DNA profile of an individual who had a DNA profile entered into the NDIS on the basis of being arrested under the authority of the United States if the individual provides a certified copy of a final court order that establishes that the charge was dismissed or resulted in an acquittal, or that no charge was filed within the applicable time period.[124] As a condition of having access to the NDIS, states must also have in place a procedure whereby the state will expunge a profile from the state's database based on the same conditions applicable to a profile being expunged from the NDIS.[125] Also, under current law the Department of Defense is required to expunge the DNA profile of an individual who had a DNA profile entered into the NDIS on the basis of being convicted of a qualifying military offense (see below) if the individual provides a certified copy of a final court order showing that the conviction was overturned.[126]

(...continued)

of Justice Reauthorization Act of 2005 (P.L. 109-162) amended the authorizing legislation for the NDIS to allow analyses of samples collected from arrestees to be included in the NDIS.

[121] According to the FBI, the American Society of Crime Laboratory Directors/Laboratory Accreditation Board (ASCLD/LAB) and Forensic Quality Services, Inc. (FQS) meet the definition specified at 42 U.S.C. §14132(b)(2)(A) for an accrediting organization. CODIS Fact Sheet.

[122] 42 U.S.C. §14132(b).

[123] 42 U.S.C. §14132(d)(1)(A)(i).

[124] 42 U.S.C. §14132(d)(1)(A)(ii).

[125] 42 U.S.C. §14132(d)(2)(A)(i).

[126] 10 U.S.C. §1565(e).

Collection of DNA Samples from Certain Federal, District of Columbia, and Military Offenders

Under current law,[127] the Attorney General is permitted to collect DNA samples from "individuals who are arrested, facing charges, or convicted of a crime or from non-United States citizens who are detained under the authority of the United States."[128] In addition, the Bureau of Prisons (BOP) is required to collect a DNA sample from each federal prisoner who is, or has been, convicted of a felony, a sexual abuse crime under chapter 109A of title 18 of the U.S. Code, a crime of violence,[129] or any attempt or conspiracy to commit any of these crimes.[130] Federal probation offices responsible for supervising individuals on probation, parole, or supervised release are required to collect DNA samples from individuals who are, or have been, convicted of any of the crimes outlined above.[131] Collected samples are required to be submitted to the FBI for analysis and their resulting DNA profiles are included in the NDIS.[132]

Current law contains similar provisions regarding the collection of DNA samples from District of Columbia offenders. BOP is required to collect a DNA sample from each prisoner who is, or has been, convicted of a qualifying District of Columbia offense.[133] In addition, the Court Services and Offender Supervision Agency for the District of Columbia is required to collect DNA samples from individuals on probation, parole, or supervised release, who are, or have been, convicted of any qualifying District of Columbia offense.[134] The government of the District of Columbia may determine which offenses under the District of Columbia Code are considered qualifying offenses for the purposes of supplying a DNA sample.[135] Collected samples must be submitted to the FBI for analysis and their resulting DNA profiles are included in the NDIS.[136]

---

[127] 42 U.S.C. §14135a(a)(1)(A).

[128] The DNA Analysis Backlog Elimination Act of 2000 (P.L. 106-546) required BOP and U.S. probation offices to collect DNA samples from anyone in their custody who was convicted of qualifying federal offenses. The act defined a "qualifying federal offense" as murder, voluntary manslaughter, or other offenses relating to homicide; an offense relating to sexual abuse, sexual exploitation or other abuse of children, or transportation for illegal sexual activity; an offense relating to peonage or slavery; kidnapping; an offense relating to robbery or burglary; any offense committed in Indian country relating to murder, manslaughter, kidnapping, maiming, a felony sexual abuse offense, incest, arson, robbery, or burglary; or any attempt or conspiracy to commit any of these crimes. The Uniting and Strengthening America by Providing Appropriate Tools Required to Intercept and Obstruct Terrorism (USA PATRIOT) Act of 2001 (P.L. 107-56) expanded the definition of "qualifying federal offense" to include crimes of terrorism, crimes of violence, or any attempt or conspiracy to commit either crime. The Justice for All Act of 2004 (P.L. 108-405) amended the definition of "qualifying federal offense" to include any felony, sexual abuse offense, crime of violence, or attempt or conspiracy to commit any of these crimes. The Violence Against Women and Department of Justice Reauthorization Act of 2005 (P.L. 109-162) authorized DOJ to collect DNA samples from arrestees and non-citizens who are detained under the authority of the United States. The Adam Walsh Child Protection and Safety Act of 2006 (P.L. 109-248) authorized DOJ to also collect DNA samples from individuals facing charges in addition to those who have been arrested or convicted.

[129] As defined at 18 U.S.C. §16.

[130] 42 U.S.C. §14135a(a)(1)(B).

[131] 42 U.S.C. §14135a(a)(2).

[132] 42 U.S.C. §14135a(b).

[133] 42 U.S.C. §14135b(a)(1).

[134] 42 U.S.C. §14135b(a)(2).

[135] 42 U.S.C. §14135b(d).

[136] 42 U.S.C. §14135b(b). The following are considered qualifying offenses under the D.C. Code: (1) any felony; (2) any offense for which the penalty is greater than one year imprisonment; (3) lewd, indecent, or obscene acts knowingly committed in the presence of a child under 16 years of age (D.C. Code §22-1312(b)); (4) certain obscene activities (continued...)

Under current law,[137] the DOD is required to collect DNA samples from each member of the Armed Forces who is, or has been, convicted of an offense under the Uniform Code of Military Justice for which a sentence of confinement of more than one year can be imposed, or of any other offense under the Uniform Code of Military Justice that is comparable to the offenses for which a DNA sample can be collected from a federal offender (see above).[138] DOD is required to conduct an analysis of the collected sample and submit the results to the FBI for inclusion in the NDIS.[139]

Post-conviction DNA Testing

The Justice for All Act of 2004 (P.L. 108-405) established procedures for post-conviction DNA testing in federal courts. Under current law,[140] upon a written motion from an individual sentenced for a federal offense (hereafter, "applicant"), the court must order DNA testing of evidence if all of the following apply:

- The applicant asserts, under penalty of perjury, that the applicant is actually innocent of the federal crime for which the applicant was sentenced, or another federal or state offense, if (1) "the evidence was entered during a federal death sentence hearing and exoneration for the offense would entitle the applicant to a reduced sentence or a new sentencing hearing;" or (2) "in the case of a [s]tate offense, the applicant demonstrates that there is no adequate remedy under [s]tate law to permit DNA testing of the ... evidence ... and, to the extent available, the applicant has exhausted all remedies available under [s]tate law for requesting DNA testing of ... evidence."

- The specified evidence to be tested was secured in relation to the investigation or prosecution of the federal or state crime for which the applicant claims to be innocent.

- The evidence to be tested (1) "was not previously subjected to DNA testing, and the applicant did not knowingly and voluntarily waive the right to request DNA testing of the evidence in a court proceeding after the date of enactment of the [Justice for All Act of 2004 (October 30, 2004)] or [did not] knowingly fail to request DNA testing of the evidence in a prior motion for post-conviction DNA testing;" or (2) "was previously subjected to DNA testing and the applicant requests DNA testing using a new method or technology that is substantially more probative that prior testing."

(...continued)

involving minors (D.C. Code §22-2201); (5) sexual performances using a minor (D.C. Code §22-3102); (6) misdemeanor sexual abuse (D.C. Code §22-3006); (7) misdemeanor sexual abuse of child or a minor (D.C. Code §22-3010.01); or (8) any attempt or conspiracy to commit any of theses crimes. D.C. Code §22-4151.

[137] 10 U.S.C. §1565(a)(1).

[138] The requirement to collect DNA samples for people convicted of certain offenses under the Uniform Code of Military Justice is separate from the DNA samples the Department of Defense collects to aid in the identification of human remains.

[139] 10 U.S.C. §1565(b).

[140] 18 U.S.C. §3600(a).

- The evidence to be tested "is in the possession of the [g]overnment and has been subject to a chain of custody and retained under conditions sufficient to ensure that such evidence has not been substituted, contaminated, tampered with, replaced, or altered in any respect" that would affect the DNA testing.

- The proposed DNA testing is "reasonable in scope, uses scientifically sound methods, and is consistent with accepted forensic practices."

- The applicant "identifies a theory of defense that is not inconsistent with an affirmative defense presented at trial and would establish the actual innocence of the applicant."

- If the applicant was "convicted following a trial, the identity of the perpetrator was at issue in the trial."

- The proposed DNA testing may produce new material evidence that would support the affirmative defense theory presented at trial and raise a reasonable probability that the applicant did not commit the crime.

- The applicant certifies that he or she will provide a DNA sample for comparison purposes.

- The motion is made in a timely fashion.[141]

If the court orders DNA testing, the testing is carried out by the FBI.[142] However, the court can order DNA testing to be conducted by another "qualified laboratory if the court makes all necessary orders to ensure the integrity of the ... evidence and the reliability of the testing process and results."[143] The cost of any DNA testing is borne by the applicant, unless the applicant is indigent; in that case, the cost of the DNA testing is borne by the government.[144]

Test results relating to the DNA sample provided by the applicant are to be included in the NDIS.[145] If the test results ordered by the court are "inconclusive or show that the applicant was the source of the tested evidence, the applicant's DNA profile may be retained in the NDIS."[146] Moreover, if the test results show that the applicant was not the source of the tested evidence, and a comparison of the applicant's DNA profile with other forensic profiles in the NDIS result in a match, DOJ is to contact the appropriate agency and preserve the applicant's DNA sample.[147]

---

[141] There is a rebuttable presumption of timeliness if the motion is made within 60 months of the enactment of the Justice for All Act of 2004 (October 30, 2004) or within 36 months of conviction, whichever comes later. The presumption of timeliness may be rebutted upon a showing that the applicant's motion for DNA testing is based solely upon information used in a previously denied motion or of clear and convincing evidence that the applicant's filing is done solely to cause delay or harass. For any motion that is not made within 60 months of the enactment of the Justice for All Act of 2004 or within 36 months of conviction, there is a rebuttable presumption against timeliness. The presumption against timeliness can be rebutted upon the court's finding (1) that the applicant was or is incompetent and such incompetence substantially contributed to the delay in the applicant's motion for a DNA test; (2) the evidence to be tested is newly discovered DNA evidence; (3) that the applicant's motion is not based solely upon the applicant's own assertion of innocence and, after considering all relevant facts and circumstances surrounding the motion, a denial would result in a manifest injustice; or (4) upon good cause shown. 18 U.S.C. §3600(a)(10)(B).

[142] 18 U.S.C. §3600(c)(1).

[143] 18 U.S.C. §3600(c)(2).

[144] 18 U.S.C. §3600(c)(3).

[145] 18 U.S.C. §3600(e)(2).

[146] 18 U.S.C. §3600(e)(3)(A).

[147] 18 U.S.C. §3600(e)(3)(B).

However, if the test results exclude the applicant as the source of the tested evidence, and a comparison between the applicant's DNA profile and forensic profiles in the NDIS does not result in a match, DOJ must destroy the applicant's DNA sample and ensure that the applicant's DNA profile is not stored in the NDIS if there is no other legal authority to retain the profile in the NDIS.[148]

If the results of the DNA test are inconclusive, the court can order further testing, if appropriate, or it can deny the applicant relief.[149] If the results of the DNA test demonstrate that the applicant was the source of the evidence tested, the applicant is denied relief, and on a motion of the government, the court can determine whether the applicant's claim of actual innocence was false. If the court finds the claim was false, it can

- hold the applicant in contempt of court;

- assess against the applicant any cost of DNA testing;

- forward the findings to BOP, who may wholly, or in part, deny the applicant's good conduct time;[150]

- if the applicant is eligible for parole, forward the finding to the U.S. Parole Commission so the commission can deny parole on the basis of the finding; or

- if the test results relate to a state offense, forward the findings to the appropriate state official.[151]

Under current law, if the applicant is convicted for making false assertions relating to post-conviction DNA testing, the applicant is to be sentenced to no less than three years imprisonment, to run consecutively with any other term of imprisonment the applicant is serving.[152]

If the results of the DNA testing demonstrate that the applicant was not the source of the tested evidence presented as a part of the case against the applicant, the applicant can file a motion for a new trial or resentencing, as appropriate, notwithstanding any law that would bar the motion as untimely.[153] Under current law, the applicant would be granted a new trial or resentencing, if the DNA results, when considered with all other evidence in the case (regardless of whether such evidence was introduced at trial), establish by compelling evidence that a new trial would result in an acquittal of the federal offense the applicant is currently sentenced for, or in the case of resentencing, if evidence of a federal or state offense was admitted during a federal death sentencing hearing and exoneration for the offense would entitle the applicant to a reduced sentence or a new sentencing hearing.[154]

---

[148] 18 U.S.C. §3600(e)(3)(C).

[149] 18 U.S.C. §3600(f)(1).

[150] Each prisoner serving a term of imprisonment of more than one year, but not prisoners serving a life sentence, can receive a good time credit of up to 54 days per year to count toward serving the sentence. The amount of the credit is subject to the determination of BOP. 18 U.S.C. §3624(b).

[151] 18 U.S.C. §3600(f)(2).

[152] 18 U.S.C. §3600(f)(3).

[153] 18 U.S.C. §3600(g)(1).

[154] 18 U.S.C. §3600(g)(2).

Preservation of Biological Evidence

The Justice for All Act of 2004 (P.L. 108-405), among other things, established standards for the preservation of biological evidence by the government. Under current law,[155] the federal government is required to preserve biological evidence[156] that was secured in the investigation or prosecution of a federal offense, if a defendant was imprisoned for the offense, unless[157]

- "the court denied a request or motion for DNA testing [of the evidence] and no appeal is pending";

- the defendant "knowingly and voluntarily waived the right to request DNA testing [of the evidence] in a court proceeding conducted after the date of enactment of the [Justice for All Act of 2004 (October 30, 2004)]";

- "after a conviction becomes final and the defendant has exhausted all opportunities for direct review of the conviction, the defendant is notified that the evidence may be destroyed and the defendant does not file a motion [for post-conviction DNA testing] within 180 days of receipt of notice";

- "the evidence must be returned to its rightful owner, or it is of such size, bulk, or physical character as to render retention impracticable and the [g]overnment takes reasonable measures to remove and preserve portions of the evidence sufficient to permit future DNA testing"; or

- the evidence has been the subject of post-conviction DNA testing (see above) and the results of the testing demonstrate that the defendant was the source of the evidence.

Grants for DNA-Related Programs

Several grant programs provide assistance to state and local governments for forensic sciences. A bulk of the programs focus on providing state and local governments with funding to reduce the backlog of forensic and convicted offender samples waiting to be processed and entered into the NDIS. However, some grant programs provide funding for other purposes, such as offsetting the cost of providing post-conviction DNA testing. This section of the report provides a brief overview of grants for forensic sciences.

Debbie Smith DNA Backlog Grant Program

The Debbie Smith DNA Backlog Grant Program (hereafter, "Debbie Smith grants") provides grants to state and local governments for five major purposes: (1) conducting analyses of DNA samples collected under applicable legal authority for inclusion in the NDIS, (2) conducting analyses of forensic DNA samples for inclusion in the NDIS, (3) increasing the capacity of state and local laboratories to carry out DNA analyses, (4) collecting DNA samples from people

---

[155] 18 U.S.C. §3600A(a).

[156] "Biological evidence" is defined as a sexual assault forensic examination kit, or semen, blood, saliva, hair, skin tissue, or other identified biological material. 18 U.S.C. §3600A(b).

[157] 18 U.S.C. §3600A(c).

required to submit them and forensic samples from crimes, and (5) ensuring that analyses of forensic DNA samples are carried out in a timely manner. The Attorney General is required to award funds using a formula. The formula distributes funds amongst state and local governments to maximize the effective utilization of DNA technology to solve crimes and protect public safety. The formula must also allocate funding amongst state and local governments to reduce backlogs by considering the number of offender and forensic samples awaiting DNA analysis in the jurisdiction along with the population and number of violent crimes in the jurisdiction. Current law requires DOJ to award not less than 0.5% of the total amount appropriated each fiscal year to each state and the District of Columbia. The territories are to receive 0.125% of the total appropriation. In addition, DOJ is required to award not less than 40% of the total amount appropriated for the program each fiscal year for conducting analyses of forensic casework.

Agencies receiving a grant under the program are required to certify that DNA analyses are conducted in laboratories that satisfy the FBI's QAS and are operated either by a state or local government or by a private laboratory under contract with the state or local government. Grants for conducting analyses of DNA samples collected under applicable legal authority for inclusion in the NDIS, conducting analyses of forensic casework for inclusion in the NDIS, and ensuring that analyses of forensic DNA samples are carried out in a timely manner can be made in the form of a contract or voucher for laboratory services that can be redeemed by nonprofit or for-profit laboratories that satisfy the QAS and have been approved by the Attorney General.

State and local governments receiving funding under the program are required to submit a report to DOJ with a summary of the activities carried out under the grant and an assessment of whether such activities are meeting the needs identified in the grant application, as well as other information the Attorney General may require. DOJ may award not more than 1% of grant funding each fiscal year to states, units of local government, and nonprofit professional organizations of persons actively involved in forensic science and nationally recognized within the forensic science community to help offset the cost of accrediting and auditing laboratories.

Debbie Smith grants were originally authorized under the Justice for All Act of 2004 (P.L. 108-405). This law amended the DNA Backlog Elimination Act of 2000,[158] authorizing appropriations of $151.0 million for each of FY2004-FY2009.[159] The program was reauthorized under the Debbie Smith Reauthorization Act of 2008 (P.L. 110-360), which includes authorized appropriations of $151.0 million for FY2009-FY2014. A funding history for this program since FY2006 is provided in **Table 2**.

Kirk Bloodsworth Post-Conviction DNA Testing Grant Program

The Kirk Bloodsworth DNA Post-conviction DNA Testing Grant program was authorized by the Justice for All Act of 2004 (P.L. 108-405). The act authorized the Attorney General to make grants to states to help defray the costs of post-conviction DNA testing programs. The act

---

[158] The DNA Backlog Elimination Act of 2000 (P.L. 106-546) authorized grants to increase the capacity of state and local government laboratories to conduct DNA analysis of biological samples from crime scenes.

[159] On March 11, 2003, President George W. Bush announced his DNA Initiative, "Advancing Justice Through DNA Technology," which provided "funds, training, and assistance to ensure that DNA technology reaches its full potential to solve crimes, protect the innocent, and identify missing persons." From FY2004 to FY2007, Congress appropriated funding for the President's DNA initiative, although the initiative was not authorized in statute.

authorized appropriations of $5.0 million for FY2005-FY2009. A funding history for this program since FY2006 is provided in **Table 2**.

Sexual Assault Forensic Exam Program Grants

The Sexual Assault Forensic Exam Program Grants were authorized under the Justice for All Act of 2004 (P.L. 108-405). The program provides grants for training, technical assistance, education, equipment, and information relating to the identification, collection, preservation, analysis, and use of DNA samples and evidence by medical personnel and those treating victims of sexual assault. Under the program, entities eligible to receive grants include states, units of local government, and sexual assault examination programs. The act authorized appropriations of $30.0 million for each of FY2005-FY2009. P.L. 110-360 extended the same authorized amount through FY2014. A funding history for this program since FY2006 is provided in **Table 2**.

DNA Research and Development Grants

The Justice for All Act of 2004 authorized grants for research and development for improving forensic DNA technology, including increasing the accuracy and efficiency of DNA analysis, decreasing the time and expense of conducting DNA analysis, and increasing its portability. In addition, the law authorized grants for demonstration projects to evaluate the use of DNA technology in conjunction with other forensic analyses. The act authorized funding of $15.0 million for each of FY2005-FY2009. This program has not received any appropriations since FY2006.

DNA Training and Education for Law Enforcement, Correctional Personnel, and Court Officers

Under this program, the Attorney General is required to make grants to provide training, technical assistance, education, and information regarding the identification, collection, preservation, analysis, and use of DNA samples and evidence by law enforcement personnel, court officers, forensic science professionals, and corrections personnel. The program was originally authorized under the Justice for All Act of 2004 (P.L. 108-405), which authorized $12.5 million for each of FY2005-FY2009. P.L. 110-360 extended the same authorized amount through FY2014. This program has not received any appropriations since FY2006.

Appropriations for DNA-Related Grant Programs

Since FY2006, Congress has appropriated over $100 million each fiscal year for DNA analysis and other forensic programs and activities. As shown in **Table 2**, most funding each fiscal year was dedicated to reducing DNA backlogs, enhancing crime laboratory capacity, and other activities related to DNA analysis. In FY2006 and FY2007, Congress gave the Administration discretion in how to award appropriated funding for DNA-related activities. The report to accompany the FY2006 Science, State, Justice, Commerce, and Related Agencies Appropriations Act (P.L. 109-108) stated that the appropriation was for a "capacity enhancement program including eliminating casework backlogs, eliminating offender backlogs, strengthening crime lab capacity, training of the criminal justice community and identifying missing persons."[160] Starting in FY2008, Congress continued to appropriate funding for DNA analysis and capacity enhancement, *including* Debbie Smith grants.[161] The language in the FY2008-FY2012 appropriations bills did not require DOJ to use *all* of the funding for DNA analysis and capacity enhancement for Debbie Smith grants, rather, it just had to award a portion of the funding for the programs. As such, DOJ has awarded funding it received for DNA analysis and capacity enhancement under a variety of programs, including Forensic DNA Backlog Reduction, Convicted Offender DNA Backlog Reduction, Forensic Science Training Development and Delivery, Forensic DNA Unit Efficiency Improvement, Solving Cold Cases with DNA Evidence, DNA to Identify Missing Persons, and DNA Research and Development.[162]

Table 2. Appropriations for Forensic Science Grant Programs

(Dollars in millions)

	FY2006	FY2007	FY2008	FY2009	FY2010	FY2011	FY2012
DNA-Related and Forensic Programs and Activities	107.1	112.1	152.3	156.0	161.0	133.4	125.0
DNA Analysis, Capacity Enhancement, and Debbie Smith Grants	*(103.2)*	*(108.2)*	*(147.4)*	*(151.0)*	*(151.0)*	*(125.1)*	*(117.0)*
Kirk Bloodsworth Post-conviction DNA Testing	*(3.9)*	*(3.9)*	*(4.9)*	*(5.0)*	*(5.0)*	*(4.1)*	*(4.0)*
Sexual Assault Forensic Exam	—	—	—	*(5.0)*	*(4.1)*	*(4.0)*	

Source: FY2006-enacted appropriations are taken from OJP's FY2008 congressional budget submission; FY2007-enacted appropriations are taken from OJP's FY2009 congressional budget submission; FY2008-enacted appropriations are taken from OJP's FY2010 congressional budget submission; and FY2009- and FY2010-enacted appropriations are taken from OJP's FY2011 congressional budget submission; FY2011-enacted appropriations are based on a CRS analysis of the text of P.L. 112-10; FY2012-enacted appropriations are taken from H.Rept. 112-284.

Notes: Amounts under the DNA-Related and Forensic Programs and Activities might not sum to total due to rounding.

Selected Legislative Issues for Congress

In the 1990s and the early part of the last decade, most of the debate about the use of DNA in criminal justice centered on the scope of DNA databases, reducing the backlog of DNA casework, and providing access to post-conviction DNA testing. Most of this debate faded with the enactment of the Violence Against Women and Department of Justice Reauthorization Act of 2005 (P.L. 109-162), which expanded federal collection statutes to include anyone arrested or detained under the authority of the United States. The act also expanded the scope of the NDIS to include DNA profiles of individuals arrested for state crimes. However, concerns about the backlog of DNA casework and access to post-conviction testing have persisted. In addition, new issues related to the use of DNA in criminal justice have emerged, including whether (1) DNA databases should be used to conduct familial searches, (2) sexual assault evidence collections kits

---

[160] U.S. Congress, House Committee on Appropriations, Subcommittee on Science, The Departments of State, Justice, and Commerce, and Related Agencies, *Making Appropriations for Science, the Departments of State, Justice, Commerce and Related Agencies for the Fiscal Year Ending September 30, 2006, and for Other Purposes*, Report to Accompany H.R. 2862, 109th Cong., 1st sess., November 7, 2005, H.Rept. 109-272 (Washington: GPO, 2005), p. 121.

[161] See P.L. 110-161, P.L. 111-8, and P.L. 111-117.

[162] A breakdown of awards under each of these programs is available online at http://www.dna.gov/funding/.

should be standardized, and (3) there should be national accreditation standard for forensic laboratories. Each of these issues are discussed in more detail below.

The NDIS and Familial Searching

The debate over familial searching is framed by the question of how to balance the desire of law enforcement agencies to use all available tools for solving crimes against the privacy of individuals who might fall under suspicion because they happen to be related to someone convicted, or in some cases arrested, for a crime. The success of familial searching depends on a close relationship between the someone with a profile in the database and the unknown perpetrator.[163] Proponents of familial searching cite research that indicates children of parents who have been convicted of a crime are more likely themselves to be convicted of a crime. Further, siblings who have been convicted are more likely to have other siblings who have been convicted.[164] Proponents also cite data from the Bureau of Justice Statistics (BJS) indicating that 46% of jail inmates reported that they had at least one close relative who had been incarcerated.[165] However, opponents of familial searching challenge its empirical basis. They stress that if offenders are more likely to have *convicted* relatives then their relatives' profiles would already be in the database and there would be no need to expand database searches to include non-convicted relatives.[166] Also, conviction data might not be a perfect indicator of criminal propensity. Biases in the criminal justice system, both racial and geographical, might lead certain groups of people, namely racial and ethnic minorities living in urban centers, to be arrested and convicted more than others with a similar rate of criminality. It could be possible that a law-abiding individual is more likely than a convicted offender to have a convicted relative.[167] On the other hand, many people commit crimes for which they are never arrested or convicted, so it is also possible that convicted offenders have relatives who have committed crimes for which there is no official record.

One of the primary privacy concerns regarding the use of familial searching is that it will put innocent people under "genetic surveillance" because they are related to someone whose profile is in a DNA database.[168] Proponents of familial searching argue that while an offender's family could be questioned by law enforcement as a result of a partial match, they could also come under the scrutiny of law enforcement during the course of an investigation that did not use familial searching.[169] For instance, an eyewitness viewing a lineup may indicate that one face bears a strong resemblance to—but is not actually—the perpetrator; at this point law enforcement might turn attention to a suspect's brother or other relatives. Relatives could also come under suspicion because the investigation turned up evidence of their involvement. Proponents also argue that familial searching might actually *exclude* relatives as the potential perpetrator.[170] Opponents

---

[163] Frederick R. Bieber, Charles H. Brenner, and David Lazer, "Finding Criminals Through DNA of Their Relatives," *Science*, vol. 312, no. 5778 (June 2, 2006), p. 1316 (hereafter, Bieber, Brenner, and Lazer, "Finding Criminals Through the DNA of Their Relatives," p. 1316).

[164] Ibid.

[165] Ibid.

[166] Erin Murphy, "Relative Doubt: Familial Searches of DNA Databases," *Michigan Law Review*, vol. 109, no. 3 (December 2010), p. 306 (hereafter, Murphy, "Relative Doubt").

[167] Ibid., p. 307.

[168] Suter, "All in the Family," p. 361.

[169] Greely, Riordan, Garrison, et al., "Family Ties," p. 257.

[170] Epstein, "Genetic Surveillance," p. 171.

---

counter that familial searching does not search the entire pool of suspects. Rather, it only subjects relatives of convicted offenders to potential law enforcement scrutiny; relatives of individuals who have not been convicted of, or arrested for, a crime are not at risk of becoming the subject of an investigation through familial searching.[171] Also, some opponents assert, if society has an interest in identifying perpetrators and exonerating the innocent by using a method that would subject non-convicted individuals to law enforcement scrutiny, then the most equitable and optimal mean to achieve this goal is universal DNA collection so that everyone, not just those who are related to someone with a profile in a DNA database, can share in the burdens and benefits of DNA databases.[172]

It has been estimated that using familial searching could increase the cold hit rate (i.e., a match in the database between an offender or arrestee profile and a forensic profile from a case where there is no suspect) in the United States from 10% to 14%.[173] However, opponents argue that familial searching would strain law enforcement's resources because they will have to investigate multiple leads, and in some cases all of the leads might be false-positives. Proponents counter this claim by noting that procedures could be put in place to reduce the number of leads to only the most promising ones. For example, laboratories could use kinship analysis to calculate the probability that a known offender DNA profile in the databases is related to the individual who left a DNA sample at the crime scene.[174] Y-chromosome analysis could, for instance, help determine whether a known offender in the database and the unknown suspect who left a DNA sample at a crime scene are related through male lineage and analysis of mitochondrial DNA (mtDNA) could help determine whether two people are related through maternal lineage.[175] While kinship analysis would make familial searching more efficient, DNA databases are currently not equipped to conduct them.[176] In addition, Y-chromosome and mitochondrial DNA analysis would require additional testing of both the known offender and the forensic samples.

Opponents argue that familial searching would exacerbate existing racial and ethnic disparities in the criminal justice system. African Americans and Hispanics, compared to whites, are disproportionately arrested and convicted, and since the NDIS is comprised of samples collected from individuals arrested and convicted for qualifying offenses, minorities are more likely to have profiles in the NDIS.[177] Disparities in the racial/ethnic compositions of profiles in the NDIS could mean that minority groups would be disproportionately investigated as a result of familial

---

[171] Murphy, "Relative Doubt," p. 308.

[172] Ibid.

[173] Bieber, Brenner, and Lazer, "Finding Criminals Through the DNA of Their Relatives," p. 1316.

[174] Kimberly A. Wah, "A New Investigative Lead: Familial Searching as an Effective Crime-Fighting Tool," *Whittier Law Review*, vol. 29, no. 4 (Summer 2008), p. 976 (hereafter, Wah, "A New Investigative Lead").

[175] Y-chromosomes and mitochondrial DNA (mtDNA) are considered "lineage markers" because they are passed down from one generation to the next without changing (except for cases where they mutate). The Y-chromosome is only found in males. Paternal lineages can be traced using Y-chromosome markers because a father passes his Y-chromosome on to his son. Therefore, fathers and sons and brothers will share the same Y-chromosome (except for cases where the chromosome mutates). In contrast, mtDNA is only passed from a mother to her children, therefore all siblings with the same biological mother will share the same mtDNA (except for cases where the mtDNA mutates), as opposed to the Y-chromosome, which is only shared by male siblings. In addition, children will share mtDNA with maternal relatives. Therefore, mtDNA can be used to trace maternal lineage. John M. Butler, *Forensic DNA Typing: Biology, Technology, and Genetics of STR Markers (2nd ed.)* (Burlington, MA: Elsevier Academic Press, 2005), pp. 201-204 and 247-249.

[176] Murphy, "Relative Doubt," p. 300.

[177] Suter, "All in the Family," pp. 368-370.

---

searches.[178] It was estimated that using the NDIS for familial searching could mean that approximately 17% of the African American population in the United States would be "findable" through the database, compared to approximately 4% of the white population (which includes non-African American Hispanics).[179] Disparities in who is investigated as a result of familial searching could also compound existing disparities in the criminal justice system, assuming that more investigations would result in more arrests and convictions.[180] While proponents of familial searching acknowledge that minority groups are more likely to become suspects in investigations resulting from familial searching, they argue that minority groups might benefit from the policy because crime is disproportionately intraracial, meaning that victims of crimes are more likely to be from minority groups.[181] Therefore, minority groups may be more likely to benefit from crimes being solved through familial searching.[182] Proponents have also argued that even if an investigative technique like familial searching does have a disproportionate effect on a specific group, it is not grounds to forgo the technique if it will solve crimes.[183]

Another privacy concern about the use of familial testing is that it could disrupt families. Specifically, opponents of familial searching have voiced concerns that someone might learn that (1) a relative had an unknown criminal history, (2) there is an existing unknown biological relationship between two people, or (3) there is no biological relationship between two people who assume they are related. However, the threat that familial searching poses to families appears to be proportional to how thorough and discreet law enforcement is in investigating leads generated by the search. Proponents argue that family secrets would only be exposed if law enforcement reveals how and why the suspect became a target of the investigation.[184] Since partial matches only suggest that an unknown perpetrator and a known offender might be related, it is unlikely that law enforcement would be able to obtain a warrant to compel the individual to provide a DNA sample.[185] Hence, law enforcement would need to investigate the lead further and develop corroborating evidence that the relative might be the unknown perpetrator. As such, law enforcement would most likely not have to share with the subject of the investigation that the lead was generated through a familial search. In cases where a DNA sample is collected from a suspect, law enforcement should be able to test it against the forensic sample to determine if the suspect committed the crime. They would not have to let the suspect know that they are not related to the person whose profile generated the lead.[186] In addition, law enforcement can legally collect and analyze DNA samples from items the suspect discarded in an area where the suspect had no expectation of privacy (for example, saliva on a soda can the suspect threw away), which would allow law enforcement to surreptitiously exclude a suspect as the possible offender.[187] Proponents have noted that law enforcement could also uncover personal information about a suspect or a suspect's family during the course of an investigation that involved alternative types

---

[178] Ibid., p. 370.

[179] Greely, Riordan, Garrison, et al., "Family Ties," p. 259.

[180] Suter, "All in the Family," p. 370.

[181] Lazer, *Searching the Family Tree for Suspects*, p. 6.

[182] Ibid., pp. 6-7.

[183] Epstein, "Genetic Surveillance," p. 163.

[184] Ibid., p. 165.

[185] Jessica D. Gabel, "Probable Cause from Probable Bonds: A Genetic Tattle Tail Based on Familial DNA," *Hastings Women's Law Journal*, vol. 21, no. 1 (Winter 2010), p. 41 (hereafter, Gabel, "Probable Cause from Probable Bonds").

[186] Epstein, "Genetic Surveillance," p. 165.

[187] Gabel, "Probable Cause from Probable Bonds," p. 42.

of surveillance or searches.[188] Yet, despite measures taken by law enforcement to not expose any family secrets, when law enforcement investigates biological relationships, there is the possibility that previously unknown relationships might be revealed.[189]

As outlined above, Congress has delineated the scope of the NDIS in law, but the law is silent as to how the NDIS can be used to make matches.[190] In the conference report for the Commerce, Justice, Science, and Related Agencies Act, 2011 (P.L. 112-55), Congress encouraged the FBI to "undertake activities to facilitate familial DNA searches of the [NDIS] and ... consider the establishment of procedures allowing familial searches only for serious violent and sexual crimes where other investigative leads have been exhausted."[191] Congress also specified that the procedures "should provide appropriate protections for the privacy rights" of individuals with a profile in the NDIS.[192] While Congress has encouraged the FBI to open up the NDIS for familial searching, there are a couple of issues Congress might consider related to this. First, if a potential familial match is made using the NDIS, should law enforcement be required to conduct additional testing before the lead is investigated further (such as Y-chromosome and mtDNA testing of both the forensic and offender DNA samples or searching public records to determine if the offender and the suspect are related)? Second, should there be additional funding for the FBI or the Office of Justice Programs to provide training to law enforcement on how to investigate leads resulting from familial matching so as to decrease any risk of accidently revealing family secrets?

Reducing the Backlog

The reduction of the backlog of DNA samples awaiting analysis has been the subject of concern in this and previous Congresses.[193] If Congress chooses to consider legislation to reduce the size of the DNA backlog, two options it might consider are increasing the capacity of state and local laboratories to conduct DNA analyses and facilitating partnerships between public and private laboratories.

---

[188] Suter, "All in the Family," p. 328.

[189] Lazer, *Searching the Family Tree for Suspects*, p. 6.

[190] H.R. 6011, the Utilizing DNA Technology to Solve Cold Cases Act of 2010 (111th Congress) would have required the Attorney General to adopt policies and procedures to allow the NDIS to be used for familial searching. The bill would have allowed FBI familial searches to be conducted only if no identical match for a DNA sample collected from a crime scene can be identified in the offender index, and the investigation for which DNA samples are collected involves murder, manslaughter, a sex offense against a minor, sexual assault, or an offense that involves a sexual act or sexual contact with another and is punishable by imprisonment for more than one year.

[191] U.S. Congress, House Committee on Appropriations, *Agriculture, Rural Development, Food and Drug Administration, and Related Agencies Programs for the Fiscal Year Ending September 30, 2012, and for Other Purposes*, Conference Report to Accompany H.R. 2112, 112th Cong., 1st sess., November 14, 2011, H.Rept. 112-284 (Washington: GPO, 2011), p. 238.

[192] Ibid.

[193] See, for example, in the 112th Congress, H.R. 1523, the Sexual Assault Forensic Evidence Registry (SAFER) Act of 2010; S. 250, the Justice for All Reauthorization Act of 2011; and S. 254, the Justice for Survivors of Sexual Assault Act of 2011. In the 111th Congress, see H.R. 2462, the Convicted Child Sex Offender DNA Index System Support Act; H.R. 4114 and S. 2736, the Justice for Survivors of Sexual Assault Act of 2009; H.R. 6085, the Sexual Assault Forensic Evidence Registry (SAFER) Act of 2010; and H.R. 6214, the Justice for Rape Victims and Improving Use of DNA Evidence Act of 2010.

Enhancing the Capacity of State and Local Laboratories

As described above, Debbie Smith grants can be used by state and local laboratories to reduce offender and forensic casework backlogs and enhance their capacity to conduct DNA analyses. This program represents the primary mechanism by which Congress has promoted efforts to reduce the DNA backlog. A study of DNA backlogs in 2007 found that there is a need for Debbie Smith grants. Of the laboratories responding to the survey, 83% replied that they would expect an increase in forensic casework backlogs if they did not receive Debbie Smith grants.[194] Moreover, nearly 90% of laboratories responded that state and local funding would not be sufficient if they did not receive federal support.[195] The study also found that while laboratories are better prepared to process offender and arrestee samples, they still rely on federal funding to conduct these analyses. Nearly 61% of responding laboratories reported that they would expect an increase in offender and arrestee sample backlogs if they no longer received Debbie Smith grants.[196] However, it is possible that respondents to the survey overstated the need for federal support out of fear that federal funding for DNA backlogs could be curtailed or eliminated if there was not a large demand for it. Using data collected as a part of the 2005 census of publicly funded crime laboratories, BJS estimated that based on the average productivity of an analyst in 2005, laboratories performing DNA analyses would have needed 73% more staff to achieve a 30-day turnaround time on all DNA analysis requests they received.[197] While it is possible that crime laboratories have hired additional analysts since 2005 and advances in technology have enabled analysts to process more requests than they once did, the demand for DNA analysis has never been greater and backlogs persist. This means that BJS's findings that crime laboratories have a need for more analysts to complete casework are most likely still valid.

Congress may choose to consider the role the federal government should play in reducing state DNA backlogs. Large backlogs can delay the resolution of criminal investigations, and Congress might have an interest in ensuring that as many criminals as possible are apprehended. As discussed above, it appears that laboratories rely on federal funding to help reduce backlogs, especially forensic casework backlogs. In addition, even though Congress has appropriated approximately $785 million for backlog reduction and laboratory capacity enhancement programs since FY2006 (see **Table 2**), data show that backlogs of offender and forensic casework are persistent. As outlined above, states have expanded the pool of people who are required to submit DNA samples, and law enforcement agencies have started to collect biological evidence in more cases. But the increasing demand for DNA analysis has not been met with increased capacity to conduct the analyses. One policy option policymakers could consider is increasing authorized appropriations for the Debbie Smith grants over the current $151 million per fiscal year.[198] While providing additional funding to states for backlog reduction could allow them to hire more analysts to work on reducing the backlog, it is likely that it would take some time to bring the backlog down from current levels. It can take up to one year to recruit, interview, and hire a new analyst; and it can take another year or two until the analyst is fully trained.[199] In addition, the workloads of more experienced analysts might actually decrease when new analysts are hired

---

[194] *2007 DNA Evidence and Offender Analysis Measurement*, p. 9.

[195] Ibid.

[196] Ibid., p. 13.

[197] *Census of Publicly Funded Forensic Crime Laboratories*, p. 7.

[198] S. 250, the Justice for All Reauthorization Act of 2011, would, among other things, extend the currently authorized funding for the Debbie Smith DNA Backlog Grant program ($151 million per fiscal year) to FY2016.

[199] *Evaluation of the Impact of the Forensic Casework DNA Backlog Reduction Program*, p. 50.

because the more experienced analysts will have to train and review the work of the new analysts.[200] Congress might also consider whether to allow Debbie Smith grants to be used for capital investments, such as new construction to expand crime laboratories. Hiring additional staff might ultimately help reduce DNA backlogs, but there could be a limit on the number of staff crime laboratories can hire given space constraints.

However, while Congress might have an interest in helping states resolve their backlogs of DNA samples, there might be some concern that by relying on federal funding to support the operations of state and local laboratories, state and local administrators would be unaware of laboratories' true funding needs, which would prevent them from seeking permanent funding solutions. It could be argued that states have contributed to the backlog problem by expanding DNA collection statutes before increasing their capacity to process the samples they were already collecting. DNA backlogs are not a static phenomenon, they will continue to increase or decrease depending on the demand for DNA analysis and the ability of crime laboratories to conduct the requested analyses. Therefore, the backlog cannot simply be eliminated by providing enough funding to state and local crime laboratories to analyze the number of samples in their backlog for any given point in time; the backlog will only be eliminated when capacity is adequate to meet demand. This means that unless state and local governments make the required investment in crime laboratory capacity, they will likely need continued federal funding to manage backlogs. Congress could consider phasing-out funding for the program to provide states with an incentive to invest in increasing and maintaining their capacity to conduct DNA analyses. Congress could also consider amending the authorizing legislation Debbie Smith grants to make it a matching grant program. Another option may be limiting the number of years states could receive funding under the program so that states would have to consider revenue streams for permanently funding crime laboratories.

Congress might consider whether to modify the Debbie Smith grant program so that a greater proportion of the funding goes to reducing the forensic casework backlog. NIJ reports that demand for grants to assist with reducing the backlog of convicted offender and arrestee samples peaked in FY2007 and has decreased in subsequent fiscal years.[201] As mentioned, currently not less than 40% of the amount appropriated for the program is to be awarded for grants to conduct analyses of forensic DNA samples for inclusion in the NDIS. Given that laboratories appear to be better prepared to process offender and arrestee samples than they are to process forensic casework samples, Congress might consider amending the authorizing statute for Debbie Smith grants so that DOJ is required to award a greater proportion of annual funding for the program to laboratories for reducing the backlog of forensic casework.

Congress could also consider providing additional funding to state and local laboratories for the purchase or development and testing of new technology that will help automate more of the DNA analysis process. Automating some of the more labor-intensive parts of DNA analysis, such as DNA extraction or reviewing the results of the analysis, could help laboratories process more samples in a shorter period of time, thereby reducing the backlog. While automation might help reduce backlogs in the long run, it is unlikely that it would have an immediate effect on reducing backlogs. It can take months to implement and validate new equipment, processes, and procedures, and doing so takes personnel away from working on processing current casework.[202]

---

[200] Ibid.

[201] *Making Sense of DNA Backlogs, 2010—Myths vs. Reality*, p. 8.

[202] Ibid., p. 49.

Another consideration might be whether to provide funding to help state and local law enforcement to either hire additional investigators or offset the cost of paying overtime to current investigators so they can investigate leads generated by DNA database matches. As discussed, law enforcement agencies have identified funding for either additional staffing for cold case units or paying overtime if the agency does not have a cold case unit as a primary need for DNA-related work. However, there could be a concern that state and local governments will come to rely on federal funding for supporting cold case units rather than identifying permanent revenue streams.

Facilitating Partnerships Between Public and Private Laboratories

As discussed above, if a public laboratory outsources some casework to a private laboratory, the public laboratory must review the work of the private laboratory before it is uploaded into the NDIS, even though both public and private laboratories have to be accredited and audited in order to conduct DNA analyses that will generate profiles for inclusion in the NDIS. In many instances, public laboratories do not have additional analysts to review work outsourced to private laboratories. Hence, the requirement that public laboratories check the work of DNA profiles generated by private laboratories might discourage public-private partnerships.[203] Also, in cases where laboratories do not have adequate resources, analysts have to review DNA profiles outsourced to private laboratories in addition to their regular casework, meaning that analysts are paid overtime, which makes the cost of outsourcing the sample more expensive. Further, it takes additional time for the work to be reviewed, resulting in a delayed uploading into the NDIS.[204]

One possible issue before Congress is whether to amend federal policy to facilitate partnerships between public and private laboratories. Congress could consider amending current law so that public laboratories do not have to review the work of private laboratories that are in compliance with the QAS. This might facilitate more public-private partnerships since public laboratories would be able to upload DNA profiles into the NDIS without having to review the private laboratory's work. One potential benefit to outsourcing more samples to private laboratories is that private laboratories might be able to analyze samples at a lower cost than public laboratories. In his testimony before the House Subcommittee on Crime, Terrorism, and Homeland Security, Dr. Jeffery Boschwitz noted that the cost of analyzing DNA samples in private laboratories can be up to 50% less than the cost of comparable analyses conducted by public laboratories.[205] Dr. Boschwitz notes that private laboratories can offer lower per case costs because private laboratories can leverage economies of scale and they have invested in research and development to lower costs in order to remain competitive.[206] However, law enforcement agencies or prosecutors would have to pay private laboratory analysts an expert testimony fee to testify in court, a cost they do not have to bear when an analyst from a public laboratory testifies. This could be a significant cost for local law enforcement agencies or prosecutors in light of the Supreme Court's ruling in *Melendez-Diaz v. Massachusetts* that defendants have a Sixth Amendment right to cross-examine an analyst who conducts an analysis of forensic evidence used in the case against the defendant.[207] However, Dr. Boschwitz testified that, in his experience,

---

[203] Dr. Boschwitz is a vice president and executive officer of Orchid Cellmark, Inc., "one of the largest worldwide providers of human DNA testing." Testimony of Dr. Boschwitz, p. 81.

[204] Ibid.

[205] Ibid., pp. 82-83.

[206] Ibid., p. 83.

[207] *Melendez-Diaz v. Massachusetts*, 129 S.Ct. 2527 (2009).

most defense attorneys do not ask for DNA testing-related testimony.[208] He testified that analysts in his laboratory are asked to testify, on average, in 2% of the cases they analyze, even after the *Melendez-Diaz* decision.[209] Nonetheless, it is not known whether other private laboratories experiences with analysts being called to testify mirror those of Dr. Boschwitz's laboratory or whether trends will change in the future. Partnerships between public and private laboratories could also provide public laboratories with a temporary increase in capacity when there is a unexpected increase in requests for DNA analysis.[210] By outsourcing more work, public laboratories could increase their capacity to a level where they would be able to handle the regular demand for DNA analysis without having to develop a surplus capacity to handle occasional increases in demand. This could promote more efficient public laboratories since they would not need to hire additional staff or purchase additional equipment to prepare for instances where there is increased demand for DNA analysis.

Some advocates of reducing DNA backlogs by having private laboratories conduct more DNA analyses might propose allowing private laboratories to have direct access to CODIS. After all, private laboratories are held to the same standard as public crime laboratories. This proposal raises one of the key questions about any public-private partnership in criminal justice: are some functions of the system inherently governmental? As discussed above, in some states laboratories retain the DNA sample that is used to generate the databased profile. This is done so that samples can be retested to confirm matches made using CODIS and to allow laboratories to retest samples in case of any technological advancements. If private laboratories were allowed direct access to CODIS, it might raise a question about whether it would be prudent for private laboratories to retain DNA samples. Another consideration might be whether involving private laboratories in investigating criminal offenses could decrease the efficiency of the investigation. When a match is made between a forensic and offender profile, there are several additional steps that must take place before charging the suspect with the crime. These steps include, but are not limited to,

- obtaining the personal identification of the subject whose DNA profile matches the forensic profile,

- verifying whether the person is the correct sex and in the appropriate age range to be the perpetrator,

- confirming that the suspect was not in custody at the time of the offense and had access to the crime scene when the offense occurred,

- corroborating the match between the offender and forensic profiles after collecting a new sample from the suspect, and

- determining if other non-DNA evidence supports or refutes that the person could be a viable suspect.[211]

While private laboratories would be able to verify the match between forensic and sample profiles, it is likely that law enforcement would have to be involved with the other steps in moving from a cold hit to a criminal charge. The coordination between the private laboratory and

---

[208] Testimony of Dr. Boschwitz, p. 83.

[209] Ibid.

[210] Ibid., p. 84.

[211] Ranajit Chakroborty and Jianye Ge, "Statistical Weight of a DNA Match in Cold-hit Cases," *Forensic Science Communications*, vol. 11, no. 3 (July 2009).

law enforcement could be complicated if the private laboratory is in another city or even another state. Policymakers might consider whether cold hits could be investigated more efficiently if the analysis was done "in-house."

There could be some concern that private laboratories might cut corners as a way to increase profit margins, thereby resulting in flawed DNA profiles being included in the NDIS. While this is a valid concern—after all, flawed DNA profiles could mean that a crime goes unsolved or that the wrong person is convicted for the crime—thus far there has not been an evaluation of whether private laboratories are more likely than public laboratories to make mistakes in their analysis. Before deciding on whether to allow public laboratories to forego reviewing DNA profiles generated by private laboratories, or granting private laboratories access to CODIS, Congress could consider requiring an independent evaluation of whether private laboratories that are in compliance with the conditions of the QAS make errors at a different rate than that of public laboratories.

Annual Backlog Data

As discussed, there is a lack of comprehensive annual data on the size of the forensic casework and offender and arrestee sample backlogs. The data collected by NIJ only provide an estimate of the national forensic casework backlog. They do not include a state-by-state breakdown of the backlog, nor do they estimate the nature of the backlog. Having reliable data on the size and nature of the DNA backlog could provide policymakers with information about the efficacy of existing policies, and it could assist policymakers if they choose to consider other policies for reducing the backlog.

Policymakers might consider creating a system to collect annual DNA backlog data. Currently, state and local governments that receive Debbie Smith grants are required to submit an annual report to DOJ that contains a summary of the activities carried out using grant funds and any other information DOJ might require;[212] but state and local governments are not required to submit data on backlogs, unless required by DOJ. If Congress chooses to consider legislation related to this issue, it might consider requiring states to report data on the size of their forensic casework and offender and arrestee (if applicable) sample backlogs as a condition of receiving Debbie Smith grants.[213] Congress could also consider reducing a state's allocation under the Edward Byrne Memorial Justice Assistance Grant (JAG) program (which provides assistance to state and local law enforcement for a variety of purposes) if a state did not submit annual backlog data to DOJ.[214] One advantage of these methods is that it provides a financial incentive for states to report backlog data. However, there might be a concern about making a state ineligible for

---

[212] 42 U.S.C. §14135(f).

[213] S. 250, the Justice for All Reauthorization Act of 2011, would, among other things, require state and local governments receiving grants to submit annual data on the current backlog for DNA casework within the jurisdiction in which the funds are used. The bill would require DOJ to publish the data submitted by state and local governments. S. 254, the Justice for Survivors of Sexual Assault Act of 2011, would, among other things, amend the authorizing legislation for the Debbie Smith DNA Backlog Grant program to require state and local laboratories that receive funding under the program to submit data to DOJ on the number of sexual assault cases that are in a backlog for DNA case work.

[214] For more information on the JAG program, see CRS Report RS22416, *Edward Byrne Memorial Justice Assistance Grant (JAG) Program*, by Nathan James.

Debbie Smith grants or reducing a state's allocation under the JAG program since funding under both programs can be used to help reduce DNA backlogs.[215]

Congress could consider requiring BJS to conduct an annual survey of publicly funded crime laboratories to collect data on DNA backlogs. One advantage to this method is that it would not make a state ineligible for funding that could be used for DNA analysis. On the other hand, it would rely on states to voluntarily provide the data. There might be concern on the part of some policymakers that states will not submit backlog data unless there is a reason for them to do so. The concern is not unfounded because response rates to surveys can vary. However, surveys conducted by BJS tend to have high response rates. For example, 90% of laboratories contacted by BJS to participate in the 2005 Survey of Publicly Funded Forensic Crime Laboratories responded to the survey.[216]

If policymakers choose to establish a system for collecting data on DNA backlogs, they might also consider the scope of the data collected. Would states only be required to submit a count of the number of forensic casework samples in their backlog, or would they also be required to provide a breakdown of the different types of forensic casework samples in their backlog, such as the number of sexual assault evidence collection kits? Should states be required to provide data on the amount of time it takes laboratories to complete the analysis of different types of samples? Should states provide data on backlogged DNA samples for the state in total or should states be required to submit data on backlogs at each local lab that provides DNA profiles to the SDIS?

Standardization of Sexual Assault Evidence Collection Kits

As discussed, the contents of a sexual assault evidence collection kit and the protocols governing whether the kit is submitted to a crime laboratory for analysis can vary from jurisdiction to jurisdiction, which could mean that the quantity and quality of evidence collected in a sexual assault case and the probability that the evidence will be analyzed could depend in part on where the sexual assault occurred. Policymakers might consider legislation that would provide for the standardization of the contents of sexual assault evidence kits and protocols for submitting the kits to crime laboratories for analysis.

One issue before Congress is whether it wants to make adopting a standardized sexual assault evidence collection kit a condition of receiving Debbie Smith grants. Another option involves reducing a state or local government's allocation under the JAG program if they choose not to use the standardized kit. If Congress chooses to consider such legislation, one question before policymakers might be whether to specify the exact contents of all sexual assault evidence collection kits used in the United States, or whether to establish a minimum standard for kits and allow jurisdictions to add additional elements if they choose. In their national protocol for sexual assault medical examinations, the Office on Violence Against Women (OVW) provided

---

[215] The National Criminal Justice Association (NCJA) surveyed states to collect data on how states used their JAG funding in 2009. States reported that they used nearly $21.9 million of the JAG funding available to them in 2009 on "forensic sciences, crime labs, DNA analysis, and cold cases." For more information on the NCJA's survey, see http://www.ncja.org/NCJA/Navigation/PoliciesPractices/Byrne_JAG_Data/Byrne_JAG_4_Pager.aspx and http://www.ncja.org/NCJA/Navigation/PoliciesPractices/Byrne_JAG_Data/ Byrne_JAG_Spending_by_Purpose_Area_and_Project_Type.aspx.

[216] *Census of Publicly Funded Forensic Crime Laboratories*, p. 8.

---

guidelines for the minimum content of sexual assault evidence collection kits. The guidelines state that, at a minimum, sexual assault evidence collection kits should include

- a kit container which has a label with blanks for identifying information and documenting the chain of custody;

- an instruction sheet or checklist to guide examiners in collecting evidence and maintaining the chain of custody;

- forms that facilitate evidence collection and analysis, including the patient's authorization for collection and release of evidence and information for law enforcement, the patient's medical history, and anatomical diagrams; and

- materials for collecting and preserving evidence, according to jurisdictional policy, including the patient's clothing and underwear and foreign material dislodged from clothing; foreign materials on the patient's body (e.g., blood, dried secretions, fibers, loose hairs, vegetation, soil/debris, fingernail scrapings and/or cuttings, matted hair cuttings, material dislodged from mouth using dental floss, and swabs of suspected semen, saliva, and/or areas highlighted by alternate light sources); hair evidence; vaginal/cervical swabs and smears; penile swabs and smears; anal/perianal swabs and smears; oral swabs and smears; body swabs; and a sample of the patient's DNA for comparison purposes.[217]

As a part of its national protocols, OVW recommended that sexual assault evidence collection kits be standardized within a jurisdiction, and within a state if possible.[218] OVW noted it could be beneficial to develop a standardized kit for use across the country, but that "[f]urther analysis is needed to assess the benefits and disadvantages of such a kit and the feasibility of development and implementation. Some challenges could include building consensus across communities regarding best practices and obtaining buy-in from involved agencies."[219] CRS did not find any evaluations of the benefits and disadvantages of a standardized sexual assault evidence collection kit and the feasibility of its development and implementation. Before requiring states and local governments to adopt a standardized sexual assault evidence collection kit as a condition of receiving funding under certain programs, Congress could consider requiring OVW or another DOJ agency to evaluate the feasibility of a standardized sexual assault evidence collection kit.

Another issue that might come before Congress is whether to reduce or eliminate funding under certain DOJ grant programs for state and local governments that do not submit all sexual assault evidence collection kits booked into evidence to a crime laboratory for analysis. One question policymakers might consider while debating this issue is whether law enforcement agencies should be required to submit all sexual assault evidence collection kits they receive. As previously discussed, there are legitimate reasons why law enforcement agencies choose not to submit collected kits to crime laboratories for analysis. Since there is currently a backlog of forensic DNA evidence, it is likely a more efficient use of a crime laboratory's time to only conduct DNA analyses on evidence where a suspect cannot be identified through other methods or where the case will proceed after the analysis is conducted. Another question policymakers might consider is whether law enforcement would be required to work through their complete backlog of sexual assault evidence collection kits. In addition to potentially adding to the backlog

---

[217] *A National Protocol for Sexual Assault Medical Forensic Examinations*, pp. 65-66.

[218] Ibid., p. 66.

[219] Ibid.

of forensic evidence, there might be some concern that analyzing old kits might have a negative effect on victims who do not wish to revisit the crime.

Arrestee Collection Statutes

As outlined above, approximately one-half of states collect DNA samples from people arrested for certain crimes. Expanding the number of profiles in the NDIS is an important element of using the database to solve cold cases. As shown in **Table 1**, as the number of offender profiles in the NDIS increased, so did the number of offenders hits and investigations aided. However, the mandatory collection of DNA samples from arrestees is still contentious. In general, courts have found that collecting DNA samples from convicted offenders is constitutional because offenders have a lower expectation of privacy, and any intrusion into an offender's privacy is reasonable in order to maintain public safety.[220] However, people arrested for crimes have a legal presumption of innocence.[221] Opponents of arrestee collection statutes argue that collecting DNA samples from arrestees is an invasion of their privacy that cannot be justified because of the presumption of innocence, meaning that arrestees do not have a diminished expectation of privacy.[222] Proponents of collecting DNA sample from arrestees argue that the state has an interest in identifying criminals and deterring crime. More specifically, they argue that there is an administrative interest in creating an unequivocal record of who has been arrested. They also suggest that people who are arrested based on probable cause have a diminished expectation of privacy because DNA can be used to identify individuals, which is not only relevant to solving the crime that the individual was arrested for, but it also provides a record of who was arrested that can be used to solve past and future crimes.[223] Arrestee collection statutes have been challenged in court, with some courts striking down the laws and other courts upholding them.[224]

Congress could consider whether it wants to promote statutes that require DNA samples to be collected from individuals arrested for certain offenses. The debate about whether to encourage states to collect DNA from arrestees is framed on one side by an interest in expanding DNA databases to include more profiles in the hope of generating more investigative leads, and on the other side by a concern about collecting more samples for analysis at a time when there is a persistent backlog of casework for analysis. If Congress chooses to consider legislation that would encourage states to adopt arrestee collection statutes, one policy option Congress could consider is providing additional funding to states to offset the cost of implementing such statutes.[225] This could be accomplished by either creating a new grant program that would provide grants to states that already have or pass arrestee collection statutes or amending the authorizing legislation for an existing grant program (the JAG program, for example) so that states receive additional funding if they already have or pass arrestee collection statutes. Congress could also consider making states ineligible to receive funding under an existing grant program, or reducing the state's funding under an existing program, unless the state has a law that requires the collection of DNA samples from arrestees. However, given that arrestee collection statutes might

---

[220] Gabel, "Probable Cause from Probable Bonds," p. 28.

[221] Suter, "All in the Family," p. 311.

[222] Ibid., p. 339.

[223] Ibid.

[224] Ibid., pp. 340-341.

[225] Two bills, H.R. 988 and S. 517, the Katie Sepich Enhanced DNA Collection Act of 2011, would, among other things, provide funding to states that collected DNA samples from people arrested for certain crimes.

be challenged in court, if Congress chooses to consider this option for promoting arrestee collection statutes it might also consider exempting states from penalties if the state's arrestee collection statute is ruled unconstitutional.

Access to Post-conviction Testing

As discussed, nearly all states have laws that provide prisoners access to post-conviction DNA testing. However, the standards for gaining access to post-conviction DNA testing vary from state to state. A provision in the Justice for All Act of 2004 (P.L. 108-405) requires that applicants for funding under the DNA Research and Development Grants; DNA Training and Education for Law Enforcement, Correctional Personnel, and Court Officers; and the Kirk Bloodsworth Post-conviction DNA Testing Grant programs demonstrate that the state provides adequate procedures for providing post-conviction DNA testing for individuals under a sentence of imprisonment or death and preservation of biological evidence. However, the incentive for states to put such procedures in place might be diminished by the fact that Congress has not provided funding for either the DNA Research and Development Grants or the DNA Training and Education for Law Enforcement, Correctional Personnel, and Court Officers programs since FY2006. Further, funding for the Kirk Bloodsworth Post-conviction DNA Testing Grant program has averaged $4.6 million since FY2006. Even if states do not have laws in place to provide adequate procedures for post-conviction DNA testing, they are still eligible to receive Debbie Smith grants, which accounts for most funding authorized under the act.

If Congress wants to promote greater access to post-conviction DNA testing for state prisoners, one policy option that could be considered is extending the prohibition on funding to all grant programs authorized by the Justice for All Act. Congress could consider extending the prohibition in connection with increasing funding for the Kirk Bloodsworth Post-conviction DNA Testing Grant program to help offset the cost of extending DNA testing to a greater number of prisoners. While extending the prohibition on funding to more grant programs might provide a greater incentive to states to expand access to post-conviction DNA testing, there might be some concern about prohibiting a state from receiving federal funding to reduce forensic and convicted offender backlogs and to increase laboratory capacity because the state chose a standard for access that is lower than the one set by Congress. Also, providing additional funding to states through the Kirk Bloodsworth Post-conviction DNA Testing program to offset the cost of expanding post-conviction testing might mask the actual cost of running the state's post-conviction DNA testing program. This could prevent the state from dedicating adequate resources to the post-conviction DNA testing program, which in turn could require Congress to keep funding grants in order to ensure that states are able to support post-conviction testing programs.

Federal Accreditation Standards

One issue policymakers might consider is whether there is a need for national accreditation standards for forensic laboratories.[226] Currently, nine states require forensic science laboratories

---

[226] S. 132, the Criminal Justice and Forensic Science Reform Act of 2011, would establish an Office of Forensic Science (Office) and a Forensic Science Board (Board) within DOJ. One of the responsibilities of the Board would be to recommend standards and procedures for the accreditation of forensic science laboratories and certification of relevant personnel in forensic science disciplines. After the Director of the Office received the recommendations of the Board, the Director would establish standards and procedures for the accreditation of forensic science laboratories and certification of relevant forensic science personnel. Under the bill, both the Board and the Office could consider (continued...)

in the state to be accredited.[227] However, even with the lack of state law requiring laboratories to be accredited, most publicly funded laboratories are still seeking and maintaining accreditation. BJS, in their 2005 census of publicly funded crime laboratories, found that 82% of crime laboratories were accredited, up from 71% of laboratories in 2002.[228] Furthermore, nearly all of the accredited laboratories were accredited by ASCLD/LAB. BJS reported that 78% of accredited laboratories were accredited by ACSLD/LAB.[229] In addition, as discussed above, all CODIS laboratories must be accredited and audited annually and analysts at these laboratories are required to undergo semiannual proficiency testing; however, these standards only apply to DNA analysis functions and not to any other forensics analyses the crime laboratory might conduct (e.g., ballistics testing, fingerprint analysis, or toxicology). While national accreditation standards would ensure that all laboratories are held to the same standard and they might help prevent embarrassing incidents where faulty procedures or downright deception has resulted in erroneous DNA analyses, accreditation can only ensure that procedures and practices are in place that would reduce the likelihood of flawed results; it cannot eliminate them. Even if a laboratory is accredited, it is still possible that human error or malignant intentions would mean that the results of some DNA analyses are incorrect. It is also possible that a private accrediting organization like ACSLD/LAB would be able to amend its accreditation standards faster to reflect changes in technology or practice than a federal board could, especially one that is charged with overseeing accreditation standards for all forensic crime laboratories.

All laboratories that receive Debbie Smith grants are required to adhere to the FBI's QAS, which requires the laboratories to be audited annually to ensure that they adhere to the QAS and requires analysts to undergo semiannual proficiency testing. Also, in order to receive funding under the Paul Coverdell Forensic Sciences Improvement Grant program, any forensic science laboratory system, medical examiner's office, or coroner's office (including any laboratory operated by a unit of local government) receiving grant funding uses generally accepted laboratory practices and procedures established by accrediting organizations or appropriate certifying bodies. It appears that current law would prohibit unaccredited laboratories from receiving grants under most currently funded grant programs. However, laboratories would not be prohibited from receiving funding under *all* grant programs (e.g., the Edward Byrne Memorial Justice Assistance Grant program) under which they could possibly receive support. Instead of creating a new office to promulgate and enforce national accreditation standards, Congress could consider amending current law to require state and local governments to certify that any funding they receive under any federal grant program for a forensic science laboratory has received and maintained accreditation from a nonprofit professional organization of persons actively involved in forensic science that is nationally recognized within the forensic science community.

(...continued)

whether any relevant national accreditation standards that are currently in effect would be sufficient, with or without supplemental standards, for the accreditation of forensic science laboratories. The standards would also include educational and training requirements for relevant laboratory personnel, proficiency and competency testing requirements for relevant personnel, and maintenance and auditing requirements for accredited forensic science laboratories. The bill would prohibit a laboratory from receiving any federal funding unless it is accredited and its relevant personnel are certified under the standards that would be established by the Office. The bill would require the Director of the Office, at least once every five years, to review whether a laboratory accredited under the standards promulgated by the Office is still eligible to receive federal funding.

[227] National Conference of State Legislatures, Table 6. Accreditation of Forensic Laboratories, http://www.ncsl.org/portals/1/Documents/cj/Table6AccredLaboratories.pdf.

[228] *Census of Publicly Funded Forensic Crime Laboratories*, p. 3.

[229] Ibid.

Appendix. State DNA Database Laws

Table A-1. State DNA Database Laws, Qualifying Offenses
(as of September 2011)

State	Felony Convictions			Misdemeanor Convictions		Arrests			
	All Convicted Felons	Juvenile Adjudications	Jail & Probation	Sex Crimes	Offenses Other Than Sex Crimes	Murder	Sex Crimes	Burglary	All Felony
Alabama	✓	✓		✓		✓	✓	✓	✓
Alaska	✓	✓		✓		✓	✓	✓	✓
Arizona	✓			✓		✓	✓	✓	
Arkansas	✓			✓		✓	✓	✓	
California	✓	✓	✓	✓		✓	✓	✓	✓
Colorado	✓	✓	✓	✓		✓	✓	✓	✓
Connecticut	✓		✓	✓					
Delaware	✓		✓	✓					
Florida	✓	✓	✓			✓	✓	✓	✓
Georgia	✓	✓	✓						
Hawaii	✓	✓	✓	✓					
Idaho	✓	✓	✓						
Illinois	✓	✓	✓	✓					
Indiana	✓		✓	✓					
Iowa	✓	✓	✓						
Kansas	✓	✓	✓			✓	✓	✓	✓
Kentucky	✓		✓	✓					
Louisiana	✓	✓	✓			✓	✓	✓	✓
Maine	✓	✓	✓						

State	Felony Convictions			Misdemeanor Convictions		Arrests			
	All Convicted Felons	Juvenile Adjudications	Jail & Probation	Sex Crimes	Offenses Other Than Sex Crimes	Murder	Sex Crimes	Burglary	All Felony
Maryland	✓	✓	✓	✓		✓	✓	✓	
Massachusetts	✓	✓	✓	✓		✓	✓		
Michigan	✓	✓	✓	✓					
Minnesota	✓		✓	✓					
Mississippi	✓		✓	✓				✓	
Missouri	✓	✓	✓	✓		✓	✓		
Montana	✓	✓	✓	✓					
Nebraska	✓		✓	✓					
Nevada	✓		✓	✓					
New Hampshire	✓	✓	✓	✓					
New Jersey	✓	✓	✓	✓	✓				
New Mexico	✓	✓	✓	✓		✓	✓	✓	✓
New York	✓		✓	✓	✓				
North Carolina	✓		✓	✓		✓	✓	✓	✓
North Dakota	✓	✓	✓	✓		✓	✓	✓	✓
Ohio	✓	✓	✓	✓					
Oklahoma	✓	✓	✓	✓	✓				
Oregon	✓	✓	✓	✓					
Pennsylvania	✓	✓	✓	✓					
Rhode Island	✓	✓	✓	✓					
South Carolina	✓	✓	✓	✓		✓	✓	✓	✓
South Dakota	✓	✓	✓	✓		✓	✓	✓	✓
Tennessee	✓	✓	✓	✓		✓	✓	✓	
Texas	✓	✓	✓	✓		✓	✓	✓	

State	Felony Convictions			Misdemeanor Convictions		Arrests			
	All Convicted Felons	Juvenile Adjudications	Jail & Probation	Sex Crimes	Offenses Other Than Sex Crimes	Murder	Sex Crimes	Burglary	All Felony
Utah	✓	✓	✓	✓	✓	✓	✓	✓	
Vermont	✓		✓	✓		✓	✓	✓	✓
Virginia	✓	✓	✓			✓	✓	✓	
Washington	✓	✓	✓	✓	✓				
West Virginia	✓	✓	✓	✓					
Wisconsin	✓		✓						
Wyoming	✓	✓	✓	✓					

Source: Gordon Thomas Honeywell Governmental Affairs, http://www.dnaresource.com/documents/statequalifyingoffenses2011.pdf.

Author Contact Information

Nathan James
Analyst in Crime Policy
njames@crs.loc.gov, 7-0264

www.ingramcontent.com/pod-product-compliance
Lightning Source LLC
Chambersburg PA
CBHW081231170526
45165CB00009B/3033